GW00632602

Ideology and Social Knowledge

Ideology and Social Knowledge

HAROLD J. BERSHADY

OXFORD · BASIL BLACKWELL

ISBN 0 631 14910 4

Printed in Great Britain by
Western Printing Services Ltd, Bristol
and bound at the Kemp Hall Bindery, Oxford

To the memory of my mother and sister

Acknowledgements

I wish to thank these friends for their encouragement and good counsel in the writing of this book: Henry Cooperstock of the University of Toronto, David Lavin of the City University of New York, Charles Rosenberg of the University of Pennsylvania, and Leslie Sklair of the London School of Economics and Political Science. In particular, I am most indebted to Joseph Elder of the University of Wisconsin who carefully read an early version of this study and whose expert knowledge of Parsons' thought prevented me from making many errors of interpretation; and Herminio Martins of St. Anthony's College, Oxford, with whom lengthy discussions of many of the philosophical issues contributed greatly to the clarification of my own thinking.

Contents

Introduction and Setting

I

The issues raised by the historical consciousness in the nineteenth century are no longer of much concern to us. Who remains troubled by the so-called "quicksands of history"? Does any one seek an "Archimedean point" from which the historical flux can be seen unhampered, all the varieties of men, their habits, meanings, relations, fully grasped in a single, all-embracing scheme? The very language of the questions is old-fashioned. Relativism, the challenge by which history, in whose name Marx, Dilthey, Croce, Mannheim and a host of others once shattered the claims of knowledge to a hard-won though abiding truth, is not of much interest to us anymore. We recall that relativism was an issue historically; we can even, if pressed, sketch the relativistic arguments; but very few of us are of the mood to respond to them. Our own troubles, a few failures or gaps of technique here and there, hardly leave us open to the anxiety of that time when each step taken seemed perilous—whether in pursuing knowledge or morality, politics or art—for no standard could be held authoritative against the welter of standards thrown up by history.

The last resurgence of interest in the relativity of history and culture, and it may well have been the very last, occurred in the period between the two World Wars. We can see now that this was not a renaissance of history, as some then thought; nothing fundamentally upsetting of our belief in the universality of reason was re-born. At worst, this belief was being temporarily shaken, but was not being replaced. Ortega y Gasset, writing on "History as a

System"[1] in the mid 1930s, could say, ". . . until twenty years ago
the state of this belief (in reason) had not suffered modification in
its general outline, but . . . in the past few years it has changed
most profoundly. So much is demonstrated by innumerable facts,
facts that are only too well known and that it would be depressing
to ennunciate once more". There is almost no-one left of Ortega's
generation to be depressed. And now these facts merely languish
in our archives, their poignancy barely remembered. I, who am
writing this almost two generations beyond Ortega's, and therefore
with the rest of my generation am accustomed to living in turmoil
and amidst constant outbreaks of violence, can have only a remote
sense of the shock and disillusion to which Ortega refers, a sense
produced by living with the survivors of those facts, grandparents,
parents and teachers, and having glimpsed their lives. The First
World War, the revolutions, the political turmoil and economic
depressions aroused a momentary, a twilight interest in history as
our confidence in the abilities of our techniques to solve all problems
faltered. But even as the writings of Karl Mannheim or Ruth
Benedict confirmed to part of a generation of students thirty or
forty years ago that no thoughts or standards were timeless, a
critical literature arose which sought to restore the universality of
reason and to deny the corrosion of the products of reason, and
possibly reason itself, by history. Far more important, to many
reason appears to have been vindicated practically, not theoretically,
by the dazzling eruption of technique in all areas, splitting every
problem into manageable proportions. The "American Challenge,"
as this technical prowess has been called, reaches far beyond the
techniques of organizing big-business or placing a man on the
moon. Relativism has been vanquished well enough, and the proof
of this is that almost no-one even remembers the effort to do so.

We are today obsessed with extending the conquests of science
and technique everywhere without hesitation over everything—over
society, over history, over the "mind," behavior, language, politics,
poetry, possibly over the workings of art itself. This obsession is
not simply a matter of extending the reach of technology, whose

[1] *Philosophy and History*, edited by Raymond Klibansky and H. J. Paton
(New York: Harper Torchbooks, 1963), pp. 283–322.

scope is indeed gigantic and ever-growing. It is not technology to which I am referring, and I am not expressing that common technophobia so often coupled to a hazy yearning for a return to handicrafts. I am referring to *technique,* and I follow Ellul's relativistic formulation of technique as "the totality of methods rationally arrived at and having absolute efficiency (for a given stage of development) in every field of human activity. Its characteristics are new; the technique of the present has no common measure with that of the past."[2]

Analysis; structure; the "universal" rules which govern relations between parts—these are the master terms taken for granted in the attitude towards all things studied and pursued today. The philosophers in the west who comment upon the knowledge, and occasionally the attitudes towards knowledge, of their own time are now inclined to give only passing attention to the skeptical and counter-skeptical ideas of the past. Some of the great arguments are of course reviewed: Hume's destruction of various notions of causality; Kant's analysis of the principle of causality as a necessary form of the understanding; the positivist conception of causality as a functional relation between variables; perhaps Poincaré's and Frank's revision of Kant to the effect that the principle of causality is a convention—although this threatens to re-open the relativistic and skeptical issues. But this is often a scant preface. In the United States and England especially, the major topic is frequently introduced by referring to the current conception of causality in the theory of quanta as statistical regularity. For the major topic with which many of the younger philosophers now occupy their writings on the theory of knowledge will likely be the analysis of the logical structure of scientific explanation. Although it is true that there has been a recent flurry of books and essays on the philosophy of history, we can detect in this literature and in our responses to it a

[2] Jacques Ellul, *The Technological Society* (New York: Vintage Books, 1967), p. xxv (italics omitted). There is only one commentator, so far as I know, who recognizes clearly that Ellul is no technophobe, and that his interest is not in technology, machines, and the like, but in the comprehension of how all human activities in our time have become organized and conducted. *Cf.* Robert A. Nisbet, "The Grand Illusion: An Appreciation of Jacques Ellul," *Commentary,* vol. 50, #3, August, 1970, pp. 40–44.

nostalgic if not a bored or futile attitude towards the philosophy of history in its nineteenth century sense. Do not either of these attitudes show the philosophy of history is practically dead, and this flurry to be not much more than a post-mortem of the philosophy of history, just as the attitudes of nostalgia and futility found in the novels depicting the life of various ethnic groups, and evoked in us as we read, tell us the life of these groups has already passed far beyond their depiction? In keeping with the times, the philosophical concern with history is now concentrated primarily upon the logic of historical explanation. Relativism? Skepticism? We have bypassed these things; they are of the past—curious and unsolved, but in any case, irrelevant problems. Our interests lie elsewhere. Philosophy follows life.

The brilliant achievements of science and technique in virtually every field, and the specialization of training by which such achievements are produced, have very nearly obliterated our consciousness of the relativity of standards which may serve to bring our own standards into question. Yet this consciousness is not quite destroyed. It survives in an attenuated form in the writings of some of those men and women who, rare in our time, are masters of more than one discipline, and are therefore brought to reflect upon the findings and assumptions of one discipline when these are compared with the findings and assumptions of another. The physicist who is also a historian of science, the philosopher turned anthropologist or sociologist, the artist who is occasionally a critic, the critic who is also a historian of art—here there will sometimes be a knowledge of the varied sensibilities to be found in history and divergent cultures, and perhaps also a response to the challenges such variety implies for the sensibility of our own time. There are three such challenges and responses which will figure prominently in what is to follow. I shall first briefly note them here.

There is the challenge historical and cultural variety is believed to make to the justification of the present. When the past is seen as a babble of irreconcilable voices, we are urged to give ourselves exclusively to the one voice we can truly understand, the voice of the present. We delude ourselves by thinking we can comprehend the past in terms other than those of our own time, and we risk losing the witting even sensuous grasp of the present by attempting to conceive the present in terms that are foreign to it. Our own time, the only time we in fact have, must be understood in and by its own terms.

There is the challenge historical and cultural variety is believed to make to our conception of humanity. When the past is seen as the demiurge of mankind, we are urged to find in history nothing less than the process which shapes humanity's development. Historical Reason—that sinuous notion of the relationship of past to present, present to future—must be clarified and formulated, for it is only through historical reason that all mankind's existence, and therefore our own existence too, can be apprehended, and each of mankind's phases assessed.

There is finally the challenge historical and cultural variety is believed to make to knowledge itself. When the past is seen merely as variable, we are urged to dismantle history and culture by breaking them into parts whose relations may be comprehended by universal rules. This response, the so-called analytical view, is often taken in opposition to one or the other responses to history and culture referred to above. Against the view which seeks to justify the present, for example, certain proponents of the analytical view argue that no conceptual justice is rendered any object, past or present, simply by adding our voice to the babble, for we are still left with no way of deciding which of the voices, if any, is the true one. Being in the present we certainly hear its voice more fully than the voice of any other time; but this amplitude may serve only to acknowledge the present; it does not and cannot confer upon the present any superior justification. And against the view which seeks to conceive humanity's development dialectically, certain proponents of the analytical view argue that this effort of conception involves analysis itself. For in seeking to formulate the principles of Historical Reason we must also define, distinguish, classify and oppose, and this is equally the method of analysis. Historical reason, therefore, cannot be distinguished from Analysis as a method of thought. All reason, so it is argued, is one. Being a method of thought, historical reason must not be confounded with the objects it seeks to analyze. Object and method are not the same things. Analysis progresses and reforms itself with every increment of knowledge, but history and culture show only enormous variation. It is our business to discern the structures underlying this variation, to identify the parts of which these structures are composed, and to formulate the laws which bind these parts to one another. By now "analysis" is indeed our business, so commonly pursued in various of its technical aspects that, with few exceptions, it is not an articulated view taken in response to history or theories of history but is a world view glazed upon our sights unconsciously by the mold of our own culture.[3]

Who are the exceptions? In France it is obviously Levi-Strauss whose recent writings, especially his debate with Sartre on the nature of historical reason, continue to interest many who are not anthropologists themselves. There is hardly a major journal of general commentary in the United States that has not by now carried a piece on Levi-Strauss. Levi-Strauss's arguments and learning are formidable; his debate with Sartre, at least in the United States, is still considered fashionable; his writing, even in translation, is lucid; and he speaks in a distinctively contemporary idiom, referring with approval to computer methodologies, techniques of quantification, and the like.

In the United States the analytical view fashioned in conscious opposition to theories of history, or historical conceptions of knowledge, is pre-eminently the work of Talcott Parsons, although this seems to be virtually unrecognized. There have been, it is true, general pieces on Talcott Parsons written to inform a literate public of developments in contemporary sociological thought. And

---

[3] *Cf.* Claude Lévi-Strauss, *The Savage Mind* (Chicago: University of Chicago Press, 1966) ch. 9. This is not to say that all "analysts" everywhere are in happy agreement. There is still room for controversy, sometimes quite acrimonious, as to what constitutes a "part," what a "structure." Differences on these matters may often be traced to lingering ideological persuasions. A Marxist may prefer to designate social parts as "classes," a liberal, bourgeois sociologist as "roles." However momentous such different characterizations may be, neither the Marxist nor the bourgeois sociologist may be any the less analytical. For apposite comments on "structuralism," see George Lichtheim, *NY Review of Books*, January 30, 1969, and the exchange of letters between Huaco and Lichtheim entitled "Klugscheisser," *NY Review of Books*, May 22, 1969.

occasionally a conceptually-minded political scientist or economic historian will attempt to adopt one or another of Parsons' schemes or terminologies to increase the rigor and sophistication of his own discipline. But whatever the reception to Parsons' work has been either within his own discipline or outside it, whether his work has been received favorably or unfavorably, intelligently or bizarrely, there has been practically no comprehension of the great tasks Parsons has set himself. And this lack of comprehension is in fact a minor irony of our time. I do not intend by this statement to add my own voice to the growing chorus which bewails the state of contemporary American sociology—indeed, I am frequently uncertain which is the more depressing, the discipline or the complaints. But surely the narrowness of our own understanding is revealed when the work of one of the indefatigable advocates of the analytical study of man and history, a work which seizes with consuming passion the powerful challenges to knowledge issued by the nineteenth-century philosophy of history and is therefore in a direct, though Americanized, descent from the "classical" European sociology, is so frequently condemned. The purveyors of science among the sociologists find Parsons' work too metaphysical or idealistic; whereas the critics among the sociologists—those especially who evince a concern with the interpretation of the history of modern society, and who hold up the earlier masters of sociology for us to emulate—find Parsons' work insufficiently historical, too formal or abstract. Perhaps it is Parsons' lack of ideological allegiance to either of these groups that accounts for their responses to his work—although I doubt this proposition captures much of anything that is involved. There is no question, however, that there are obstacles to the easy comprehension of Parsons' work. There is the matter of Parsons' tortuous, often elephantine style which makes access to his ideas a strenuous undertaking. Agreed. Yet, in the exposition to follow there will be exhibited many examples of Parsons' writing that are perfectly clear. There is further the fact that Parsons has written voluminously, has produced many huge tomes in an impatient age—which is perhaps why his essays are appreciated more than his books. There is also the fact that Parsons' works are heavily freighted with a scholarship to which graduate

B

schools in sociology for the past thirty years have rarely given their students more than the most fleeting acquaintance at the very best. Of greatest importance, in my opinion, is the fact that the problems and issues of deepest concern to Parsons have in large part been ignored. Possibly there is the presumption that these problems have been long resolved, for most of the emphasis is now placed upon a detail of one or another problem, or upon a technique for elucidating that detail. Yet, there is hardly any explicit recognition of the full scale of the problems to which these details and techniques may be referred and interrelated. Thus the frameworks Parsons has constructed are rarely understood to be his response to the broader problems, whereas the appearance and re-appearance of these problems in his writings is frequently greeted with bafflement, alarm, hostility or silence.

I believe that Parsons' work is a great though limited achievement, and it is my aim to define that achievement and to show its limits. However, the significance of Parsons' work does not lie in its intellectual achievements alone, whatever the greatness of those achievements may be. For Parsons' work may also be taken as an attempt to express and fix the presuppositions of a large part of our lives. Parsons' work, in other words, is a philosophy of technique, of action; it provides an analysis of the categories underlying the transformative mentality which is at the very center of our worldwide technical culture. Parsons may not have deliberately intended this; nowhere in his work is there a recitation of the details of the technical outlook such as may be found, for example, in the glum catalogues provided by Juenger or Ellul. In Parsons' work the technical details are for the most part tacitly assumed; they exist as an ambiance for which his work provides the organizing cognitive motif—just as, indeed, the details of technique are the encompassing situation we take for granted and in which we all act out our lives. To call the cognitive motif of this situation "analysis" is accurate enough, although this is an academic and, in present circumstances, a somewhat misleading way of putting it. In fact, the guiding theme of technique, the outstanding characteristic that runs through all of the technical details is something we are all much more aware of: it is, simply, action. Action, that is, not merely in the sense of our activity in the world enhanced by our tools, for this might still be taken to presuppose a distinction between the world and ourselves, between the tools we use and the objects which yet remain separate from our tools. Action means, in the wholly unprecedented scale to which we can intervene in the world and reshape the world according to our wishes, that we find only ourselves, our own wishes and our own features, wherever we may look.[4] In the sheer scope of the objects we do not merely seize but indeed *create* by our techniques, whether they are objects of "nature," such as genetic and atomic structures, or of society, such as political and personality structures, we transform them all into mere artifacts of our existence, and thus the distinction between the world of nature and the world of men is erased. The consequence is not that men have been assimilated into nature, or nature into men, as the so-called warfare between the philosophical schools of materialism and idealism would once have had it. The consequence is, rather, that the mood of the modern age is of the most radical and far-reaching subjectivism, revealing that neither a common world of objects nor a common world of men exists. In our own time, as Hannah Arendt puts it, ". . . we can take almost any hypothesis and *act* upon it, with a sequence of results in reality which not only make sense but *work*. This means quite literally that everything is possible not only in the realm of ideas but in the field of reality itself."[5]

The academic preoccupation with objectivity from the nineteenth century to the present is unquestionably linked to the anguish aroused upon the recognition of the extreme subjectivity which constitutes our mood. I will inspect certain versions of this preoccupation among historians and sociologists later. For the moment it is sufficient to say that Parsons has faced the issue of subjectivity by way of a sustained reflection which never lapses into mere dogmas or slogans upholding objectivity as the sure road to cognitive

[4] Here I follow in general Hannah Arendt's luminous discussion of the *vita activa* in two of her books: *The Human Condition* (Chicago: The University of Chicago Press, 1958) and *Between Past and Future* (New York: Meridian Books, 1963).

[5] "The Concept of History," in *Between Past and Future*, p. 87; italics in the original.

salvation. Not once does Parsons subscribe blindly to that cult of objectivity whose emergence coincided almost precisely with the dawning of our astronomical powers of action—an "objectivity" insisted upon when men have lost a world in common, and resembling in the insistence nothing so much as the formal declaration of Papal Infallibility issued by the Roman Church in 1870 when the temporal Power of the Pope had almost vanished. Given our pervasive inwardness *and* our gigantic powers, we begin to suspect that "objectivity" may be less a methodological canon than an attempt to restrict what is possible, to narrow the range of virtually infinite objects to a comparatively few privileged ones. There may be a truth to the idea currently being pressed in some quarters that there is a "politics of objectivity" despite the fact that this idea is viewed as a scandal in conventional academic circles.

Parsons seeks to find amid the great welter of views, visions, ideas and objects actual and possible, some constants, some universals in which all social thought must participate and of which all social objects must be constituted. In this way Parsons hopes to attain an insight which will hold for all men and all societies, and thus to get beyond the singularities which appear to enclose our lives. Indeed, Parsons believes the schema developed in his first major work, upon which all of his later efforts are based, has a "phenomenological status" in Husserl's sense,[6] that is, the schema is supposed to be essential to any comprehension of society, for it is utterly co-extensive with everything that may be affirmed of society. Parsons believes, then, that the schema he has brought forth is the conceptual bedrock upon which even the most diverse thinkers, whether they know it or not, find a common foundation. In the face of the subjectivity, the plurality, the conflict, the politics of thought, Parsons counterposes a supreme intersubjectivity, not an objectivity which may crumble upon the introduction of yet another new partially esteemed object.

For reasons I shall make clear throughout the text, I do not

[6] These are Parsons' words. See his comments in *The Structure of Social Action* (Glencoe: The Free Press, 1949, 2nd edition), p. 73. Parsons refers to Husserl's *Logische Untersuchungen*, the substance of which has been rendered in English and commented upon by Marvin Farber, *The Foundation of Phenomenology* (Cambridge: Harvard University Press, 1943).

believe Parsons has fully acceded to his aims, although I admire and have some sympathy for his intellectual effort. In any case, it should be obvious that the foundation Parsons wishes to establish must not favor any partisan point of view, for then there would be no foundation at all, merely another view. Part of the labor of Parsons' scholarly life has been to show how the most opposed political and philosophical views, Marxism and conservatism, positivism and idealism, partake implicitly of the schema he has fashioned. It should also be clear that if this schema is to be so ubiquitous as to be at the root, but not be a mere melange, of such disparate views, the schema must be extraordinarily general, general beyond the generalizations of any particular view. For this reason among others Parsons has deliberately gauged his schema to provide an immensely broad sweep of generalization. But on the matter of generality exactly a difficulty arises which may be insuperable. Since much of my objection to Parsons' achievement centers upon what I believe to be the incapacity of his schema to overcome this difficulty, I will first briefly sketch the rudiments of the difficulty here so that the reader may be alerted as to what is to come and also be forewarned of my own "bias."

All thought, even the most comprehensive doctrines intending to snare the entire universe, man, the earth, and the heavens—in other words, Hegel's system itself—turns out soon enough to have captured only a part at best. Did not Feuerbach show, for example, that the myriad facts of nature could not be deduced from Hegel's system, and was this lack not a mark against that system's so-called comprehensivity?[7] In similar vein, did not Marx scoff at Hegel's "concrete universal" which, so long as it remained universal, could never point to the concrete, could only refer, as Marx gave the example, to *the* fruit, the substance or essence of fruit, but never distinguish between, say, apples, pears, strawberries, almonds?[8] One need not tarry long on the fact that Hegel's all-embracing system has its limits to conclude that all thought is abstract in some

[7] *Zur Kritik der Hegelschen Philosophie* (Stuttgart, 1903).
[8] From Marx's *Die heilige Familie*. The pertinent passage has been translated by Sidney Hook, *From Hegel to Marx* (Ann Arbor: The University of Michigan Press, 1962), pp. 312–315.

measure. For all thought, whether by design or accident, always excludes some things. There is no particular dilemma to be found in the abstract character of thought so long as the concepts we use are precise enough to include and pinpoint what it is we are interested in. And with a few romantic exceptions, no one, certainly not Parsons, is any longer interested in representing conceptually everything there is. Parsons wishes to find a common bond in social thought—gargantuan enough task that this is, compounded by the difficulty of clarifying our understanding of what comprises the social. But whatever its reach, social thought is assuredly not everything. Parsons has no interest in representing nature, for example, and he makes no grandiose claims that sociology is the "queen of the sciences"—begetting and devouring every other discipline—as a few of the megalomaniacal exponents of sociology have insisted. Parsons wants to found society conceptually, to describe all social facts, and to forge a rigorous explanation of these facts. Notwithstanding the greater modesty of Parsons' aims when compared to Hegel's, and the fact that Parsons is no Hegelian by any stretch of the imagination, I believe the results of Parsons' endeavor are defficient in a manner similar to the defficiency of Hegel's system.

Parsons attempts to dissolve all individual societies into a set of characteristics and functions. These characteristics and functions, lengthy and complex as they must be, when combined in different ways are supposed to reproduce, as it were, any individual society. Since all of these items are not present in every society, Parsons has also payed some attention to the question of when certain of these characteristics and functions will or will not occur. Underlying the rather extensive panoply of items Parsons has adduced is a small, master set of highly general conditions to which Parsons believes every society must conform. The very terms by which this master set of conditions is expressed are, by virtue of their extreme generality, capable of absorbing any other social theory and re-expressing that social theory as an instance or a special case of the more general theory of action Parsons has developed. "There are no group properties that are not reducible to properties of systems of action and there is no analytical theory of groups which is not translatable into terms of the theory of action," Parsons asserts at the end of his first major work.[9] Assuming, for the sake of the argument, Parsons has been successful in this—where does the dilemma lie? The dilemma lies, I believe, in the fact that all of the characteristics and functions Parsons offers us, no matter how few or many are used, or how they are combined, cannot reproduce the features of any single society.

It is as though one were to attempt a comprehensive theory of physiognomy and had developed for this purpose a finite list of facial features and mannerisms which, when put together in different ways, are supposed to bring out any distinctive face. To keep to the figure, we would then have, let us say: noses, long or short; mouths, full or thin; eyes, small or large; brows, protruding or flat; foreheads, high or low; ears, small or large; typical expressions, taut or relaxed, happy or morose, and so on. The list could obviously be extended almost indefinitely (although in Parsons' case, he is satisfied he has produced just enough items. More on this later). Select a face you know well and attempt to "re-constitute" that face by any combination of characteristics from the list above, or some other general list of your own choosing. Do you think you have reproduced that face? Accost a stranger in the street, show him your re-constituted face, bring him into a room full of people of whom one has that face you have re-constituted. Do you think that obliging stranger will unerringly identify the living face from the collection of characteristics you have given him as the re-constituted face? He might if you have a sharp eye and have hit upon that expression, or that feature, which utterly and unmistakably captures that living face. Otherwise, your "re-constituted" face will do for any number of other faces, and doing for any number of other faces will be incapable of snaring any one. The trouble with Parsons is, and it is a pervasive trouble with much of modern thinking, he is so intent on bringing out the general characteristics of societies that whenever he portrays any individual society we are left merely with general features that are applicable as well to any number of other societies. We of course know that a woman we love is a female and shares many characteristics in

9 Parsons, *op. cit.*, p. 747. Italics omitted.

common with other females; however, it is not females we love but this specific woman. We do not yet, at least, confuse the two.

II

I do not believe the generality of Parsons' thought is a mere reflex of his ideological motives, his metaphysics, his position at Harvard, or his political and class interests, as has recently been alleged of this and other aspects of his work.[10] Far more significant for the generality of Parsons' thinking, as I will show in detail, are his concerns with overcoming the relativity of social thought and fulfilling the tenets of the conception of knowledge he holds. These are the concerns which lead him in pursuit of universals of social thought, of logical and conditional necessities for the conceiving and the occurring of any social object. And these are the pursuits, in turn, which impart to his thinking its generalized and, as it were, "timeless" cast. That the pursuits to which Parsons has given himself are not the unique by-products of his particular ideology or political interests may be seen clearly by noting that there are some who endorse similar pursuits and yet differ from Parsons on political matters. Noam Chomsky, for example, who can hardly be said to share Parsons' political viewpoint, when asked whether his view of linguistics, which suggests innate structures of the mind, leaves any role to historical determination of human needs and their fulfillment, is reported to have answered in this fashion:[11]

I think we have to be very cautious about this until we have a much broader understanding of the range and extent of possible variations in human behavior...As human beings, as living human beings, we are primarily interested in the differences among ourselves and that is perfectly proper. As a human being, living in the contemporary world, I am very much interested in the difference between English and Japanese

[10] A. W. Gouldner, *The Coming Crisis of Western Sociology* (New York: Equinox Books, 1971) esp. chs. 6 and 11.
[11] "Interview with Noam Chomsky," *New Left Review*, 57, September–October, 1969, p. 32.

because I cannot understand Japanese and it would be useful to be able to. But as a linguist I am interested in the fact that English and Japanese are rather minor modifications of a basic pattern and that other linguistic systems could be imagined which violate that basic pattern, but that they do not in fact anywhere exist ... A serious study of morals or of social systems would attempt the same thing. It would ask itself what kinds of social system are conceivable. Then it would ask itself what kinds have actually been realized in history and it would ask how these came into existence, given the range of possibilities that exist at some moment of economic and cultural development. Then, having reached that point, the next question is whether the range of social systems that human beings have constructed is broad or narrow, what is its scope, what are its potentialities, are there kinds of social system human beings could not possibly construct and so on ... Of course, there is an enormous human significance in living in one social system rather than another, in capitalism rather than feudalism, for example. Whereas there is no human significance, other than accidental, in speaking one language rather than another. But that is a different question from asking which kinds of system of social organization are possible for human beings and which kinds are not.

A "serious study of social systems," as Chomsky with characteristic acumen puts it, has exactly been the endeavor of Parsons' scholarly life.

There are a few "Platonist elements" in Chomsky's and Parsons' thought, and Chomsky has in fact written interestingly of the relation of these "elements" to his own work.[12] Should we impute to Chomsky, then, as has been imputed to Parsons, a "metaphysical vision" of the "oneness of the world"; a need to make the world "safe" in its oneness; and a mixture of "liberative" and "conservative" sentiments, akin to the sentiments presumed to be underlying Plato's philosophy of Eternal Ideas, that would limit the conception of man's freedom? Whether this concoction can be attributed to anyone's work is questionable in the extreme. The first and second imputations, for example, taken together must seem patently absurd. For if a metaphysical vision of the oneness of the world is held with any conviction, there would be no point in attempting to make the

---

[12] *Language and Mind* (New York: Harcourt, Brace & World, 1968), chs. 1 and 3.

world safe in its oneness. Inordinate deductive prowess is not required to see that attempts of this sort can obviously have no consequence. Given the "metaphysical vision," there would only be some point in attempting to fathom the oneness of the world in the face of apparently great, possibly endless, diversity. As Chomsky puts it for his conception of a "generative grammar" of language: "The speaker makes *infinite* use of finite means."[13] Chomsky has been outspoken in his concern for human freedom, and has expressed his belief in the fundamental human capacity and need for creative self-expression. But Chomsky wishes to identify the principles of any human language as distinguished, say, from animal communication systems. He has argued forcefully that the understanding of animal communication illuminates virtually none of the aspects of human language. As the principles he has formulated serve to identify a human language yet place no restrictions on the use to which any human language is put—the third imputation referred to above, of a mixture of 'liberative' and 'conservative' sentiments limiting the conception of man's freedom, would thus be, at the very least, vacuous if directed to Chomsky's work. And although the problem of the creative use of human language remains intractable to his formulations so far, this is a technical difficulty—possibly insuperable—which sheds no light on Chomsky's motivations. In any case, the analogy between Parsons' and Chomsky's endeavors should help elicit the fact that the endeavor itself need not be associated necessarily with any specific "sentiments" or "metaphysical" assumptions. If one is going to think of a human language, Chomsky has shown that it would be of some assistance to be able to distinguish that language from grunts, whistles, squeals or barks.[14] Can the mere making of this distinction be traced to a metaphysical or political motive?

In Parsons' case, the limitation upon man's conception of freedom is seen to derive, presumably, from his laying down of universal rules—"essences"—necessary for the existence of any possible society. The observation is made that Parsons conceives all social worlds operating within the *same* limits, and the objection is raised

[13] Chomsky, *ibid.*, p. 15 (my emphasis).
[14] Chomsky, *ibid.*, esp. ch. 3.

that his mere conceiving of such constant limits is arbitrary, takes
no cognizance of the future, and thus reflects a conservative sentiment.[15] For Parsons as for Chomsky, the universal rules serve to
identify a human society as distinguished, say, from a "society"
of bees. There may be a few parallels between the two orders, but
except for occasional eccentric attempts to postulate an identity
between the organization of bees and men, the virtually uniform
repetition of bee "societies" versus the sheer variability of human
societies is enough to provoke the deepest doubts that any identity
of the organization of bees and men exists. Yet, have not the studies
of historians, anthropologists and sociologists over the past two
hundred years often tacitly assumed and made us dimly aware that
there are several senses in which we acknowledge even a society
of men most alien to us as being a distinctively human society?
Before we boggle at Parsons' fomulation of universal rules, we
must at least show the rules he has conceived are too meager or
faulty to comprehend the historical diversity of social worlds that
have occurred, not to speak of possible future social worlds that may
occur. This would entail either a logical analysis of Parsons'
formulation or, to put it baldly, that Parsons' formulation be
opposed by a concept of the "social" more general and more richly
conceived than the concept he has developed. Without the analysis
or the concept, nothing could be shown. Referring to future social
worlds for which Parsons' concept would be inadequate is always
a logical possibility for any concept. But as long as these future
social worlds remain unspecified—their invocation being redolent,
perhaps, of an ill-defined "hope"—the possibility of their vague
occurrence does not constitute a critique of the concept in question.

One may object to the substance or the manner of Parsons' formulation, but each of these involve different issues entirely from the
issue implied by the fact that he provides some definition of a subject
matter. To protest the latter fact in any meaningful way would
involve recourse to an epistemological argument in which it can be
maintained without contradiction that to distinguish the subject
matter of one's study from any other subject matter is indeed

[15] Gouldner, *op. cit.*, ch. 11, esp. section entitled: "Ambivalence Toward
Society."

unnecessary. There is very little evidence, however, that the imputations under discussion proceed explicitly from epistemological considerations. Based upon the postulate of a future without content, and
an epistemology apparently inconceived, the imputations of a
conservative sentiment and a metaphysical vision simply to the fact
that Parsons gives a definition are not only as empty and misleading
as they would be to the analogous aspects of Chomsky's work, but
divert attention from everything Parsons is after. Parsons' work can
be understood less as a "metaphysics" he desires to affirm than, so
to speak, as a "synthesis of physics," a unification of social knowledge towards which he strives. I shall have occasion to comment
upon the metaphysical aspects of Parsons' thought later in the text.
For the moment, I should like simply to call attention to the fact
that much the same striving can be detected even in those who
manifestly do not endorse Parsons' so-called "metaphysical vision,"
as the following brief considerations shall bring out.

Let us grant that Parsons' ideological motives direct his gaze only
to certain aspects of society and consequently limit the range of
his thinking solely to those aspects. Let us also grant that the range
of anyone's thinking is limited by one ideological motive or another.
However, the ideological constraints upon Parsons' or anyone's
thought, interesting or urgent though their revelation is sometimes
felt to be, are apparently not considered to be utterly confining. For:
"the problem is to crack ... the viable elements ... out of the
conservative ideological structure in which they are imbedded, to
rework them thoroughly, and to assimilate them in a social theory
which is not limited and confined to the assumptions of our present
society." These are the words of one of Parsons' staunchest critics,
A. W. Gouldner, who professes to metaphysical views, an ideology,
and political interests sharply opposed to Parsons'. Gouldner avers
that Parsons has seen "most deeply" into certain problems. "Theory
and praxis" are indissoluble, he tells us, nevertheless this bond can
be surmounted. Some avenue for reconciling disparate theories
(and sorts of praxis?) does in fact exist. We can leap over the
shadows of other men by undertaking a new "praxis," for in this
way, and through a "reflexive" and "authentic" sociology,
theoretical "reconstructions" and "sublations" will issue which

would preserve the segments of Parsons' thinking where he has seen most deeply, and yet provide a vision that goes beyond his. Thus a "reflexive" sociology and a different (broader?) "praxis" would better service the ultimate cognitive goals espoused by Parsons than the services his limited "praxis" and ideologically formed contributions have been able to give.[16] By posing a "dialectical" conception of the growth and unification of knowledge, notice that Gouldner raises an issue with Parsons that bears a certain resemblance to the issue of historical versus analytical reason, referred to earlier, debated between Sartre and Levi-Strauss.

However, the nature of Parsons' theoretical venture must not be obscured from criticism by taking his ultimate goal as a given, denying by a dialectical hypothesis that he has achieved it, and gesturing towards a vacancy, a future through which it is supposed this goal would be given some measure of fulfillment. If Parsons is an important theorist—as Gouldner and many others readily acknowledge, and as I would agree—attention must be payed to his emphatic belief that he has achieved a unitary foundation for the social knowledge that presently exists. Why does he set himself this task? And of what does this foundation consist? How may we understand the sense in which 'unitary' is meant? In appraising Parsons' achievement, should we not ask whether there are things whose present discernment cannot be fully "assimilated" into an overarching conception without irreparable damage to the very discernment of those things? These are not questions that devolve obviously or necessarily into metaphysical considerations, ideological motives, matters of "praxis," or political and class interests. Parsons' conceptual achievements must themselves be understood and assessed whatever the "motivation" of his thinking may be.

III

The body of work produced by Talcott Parsons is not of one piece. The affinities that may exist, say, between *The Structure of Social Action* (1937) and *The Social System* (1951) are clearly not such

---

[16] Gouldner, *ibid.*, section entitled: "The Potential of a Radical Sociology"; and "Epilogue."

that the later work is a "deduction" from the earlier, nor is the later work simply an amendment of the earlier. Yet, the later work does not completely surprise us. It is distinctively "Parsonian" not only because it is similar to the earlier work in writing style or in degree of theoretical abstraction, although these too unquestionably give the later work its Parsonian cast, but because it maintains and develops, now in one direction, now in another, the same set of theoretical interests.

The exact definition of these interests, and whether they are indeed developed, is a matter of some question in the already vast and continually growing commentarial literature on Parsons. Devereux's and Williams' accounts, of those which are known, seem to be the clearest in their recognition of the continuity of Parsons' concerns.[17] They point to a major set of broad substantive problems which has been common to all Parsons' work and has thus given it a kind of unity: the problems of social order, social integration and equilibrium. Since each of his major works has been concentrated on different facets of these problems—as they apply to a unit act, to a system of interaction, to sub-systems in the larger social system, to the emergence of new systems—the connections between them are not so much logical or deductive as they are developmental or organic. The differences between the works, therefore, are differences in elaboration and emphasis; each one shares in a common perspective. Parsons has himself written many times of this perspective, and of its relationship to various of his works, and in 1965 again published a summary statement of his views.[18]

There are other commentators, however, who while not denying a certain continuity of Parsons' substantive concerns, are impressed with what they consider to be evidence of fundamental alterations in philosophical outlook over the course of his work—from an early nominalism to a later realism,[19] or from an early subjectivism to a

[17] *The Social Theories of Talcott Parsons* (Englewood Cliffs, New Jersey: Prentice Hall, Inc., 1961) edited by Max Black, chs. 1 and 2.

[18] "Unity and Diversity in the Modern Intellectual Disciplines: The Role of the Social Sciences," *Daedalus*, vol. 94, #1, Winter, 1965.

[19] *Cf.* Martindale, Don, "Talcott Parsons' Intellectual Development," *Alpha Kappa Deltan*, Winter, 1959, pp. 38–46.

later operationalism.[20] These alterations are alleged to have far-reaching metaphysical and epistemological consequences. On the metaphysical side, they are expressed in Parsons' changing formulations of the "units" of society. The "act" of the early work was an "atomistic particle." And since " . . . in principle all analyses performed by use of social structures could be made more precise by analysis into social actions," this emphasizes the conceptual importance of "parts."[21] The early conception is therefore deemed to be nominalistic. The slightly later work is incipiently realistic, for it takes the "actor-situation" as the unit of analysis. Greater importance is now given to the "whole," although the whole is not yet much more comprehensive than its parts.[22] But following this, Parsons is supposed to have developed into a full-blown realist. Now the unit is "the social system," and it is a whole of such magnitude that it even contains parts which do not empirically exist (some of the pattern-variable configurations), although they are of theoretical significance.

On the epistemological side, the alterations in Parsons' philosophical outlook, and their consequences, are expressed in his changing formulations of certain key terms. In the early work, it is claimed, Parsons holds to the view that the phenomena of symbolic behavior are " 'outside the range of scientific observation and analysis.' "[23] Here Parsons is opposed to an operational or empirical criterion as the sole criterion of the meaning of concepts. His conception is therefore considered to be at least subjectivistic. But in the later work he identifies the meaning of certain of his concepts

[20] Cf. Lundberg, George, Foundations of Sociology (New York: The Macmillan Co., 1939), pp. 41–42, note 19, for the imputation of 'subjectivism,' and Lundberg's later essay, "Some convergences in Sociological Theory," American Journal of Sociology, vol. LXII, 1956–7, pp. 21–27, for his comments on Parsons' change to operationalism. For the allegation of Parsons' subjectivism, see also Bierstedt, Robert, "The Means-End Schema in Sociological Theory," American Sociological Review, vol. 3, October, 1938, pp. 665–671.

[21] Martindale, op. cit., p. 41.

[22] Martindale here refers to Parsons' essay, "The Present Position and Prospects of Systematic Theory in Sociology," in Twentieth Century Sociology (New York: Philosophical Library, 1945), Gurvitch, Georges and Moore, Wilbert E. (editors), pp. 42–69.

[23] This is Lundberg's earlier statement. See Foundations, op. cit., p. 41.

with Bales's categories of interaction. Since "Bales's categories were developed in concrete, objective research and are subject to the usual empirical checks of reliability and validity . . . this gives us . . . *for the first time*, operational specifications of the meaning of (Parsons') terms."[24]

Has Parsons' philosophical outlook changed *that* much? Virtually everyone agrees, and Parsons himself has readily said, that there have been changes in his work, that he has constructed new bases upon which he has built different conceptual structures at several points during his career. But there is a unity in his work that does not come from his sustained interest in the problems of social order, social integration and equilibrium alone. This unity comes as well from another equally pervasive set of interests in problems concerning the nature of the theoretical enterprise itself. They are epistemological problems and they are of two kinds. One is the question of even the possibility of a general science of society. The other is the question of the admissibility of certain kinds of conceptualizations *in* a general science of society. To solve these problems Parsons must first show how a general science of society is possible, and second, that once possible, the science must include those very conceptualizations that have been deemed inadmissable. But he does not do this only as a philosopher would, that is, he is not content merely with showing the possibility of a science of society, for he has other interests as well. Parsons intends to provide at least some of that scientific knowledge itself, for it is the science above all other things, the scientific solution to the problems of social order, etc., that he is ultimately after. This distinction shall become much clearer throughout the exposition. But that it is one thing to show the possibility of scientific knowledge, another to produce that knowledge itself, may be noted for present purposes by the example of Kant and Newton in which these two unlike pursuits constitute precisely one of the major points of difference between their work. Parsons, however, attempts to do both things, and in this attempt he develops a certain strategy to which he adheres throughout his work. The logical form of this strategy is "a priori" and consists of a specific

---

[24] See Lundberg's essay, *op. cit.*, p. 22 (my emphasis).

manner of relating conceptual materials to each other. It is a mode of theorizing through which propositions may indeed be construed, and does not consist simply of definitions and classifications as some have argued.[25] Indeed, Parsons must adhere to this strategy so long as he believes that a deviation from it would allow the epistemological problems to be raised again. If that were to happen his entire scientific undertaking would be placed in epistemological jeopardy. Because he is satisfied he has solved these problems, and they can be solved in no other way, Parsons maintains the strategy he had first developed in his early work. And it is in *this* constancy, no less than the persistence of other features, that the "Parsonian" cast of all his work may be seen.

One of the interests of this study shall be to show that despite the shifts in his thinking, however radical they may be deemed to be, despite the new bases and structures Parsons has created, the *manner* by which he relates base to structure in all cases remains essentially the same.

The main interest of this study shall be to reveal and assess the logical nature of the strategy Parsons employs throughout his work and to inquire as to its limits. Not until that strategy or mode of theorizing is made clear may a critique of it sensibly be made. Once clear it may be subjected to a number of tests; in employing this strategy does Parsons fulfill *its* logical requirements; does this strategy accomplish the objectives intended for it; in such accomplishment are there new problems opened which cannot be solved by this strategy alone; in what senses are the objectives themselves "defensible," and, if these objectives are open to question does this not as well open to question the employment of any strategy that is used to achieve them; are there alternative strategies for the accomplishment of these objectives and how do they compare to the strategy Parsons has developed?

Even if one of the contentions of this study is correct, that the logic of Parsons' strategy has remained constant, it does not strictly follow that the strategy has been utilized in the face of a set of

[25] *Cf.* Homans, George Caspar, "Contemporary Theory in Sociology," in *Handbook of Modern Sociology* (Chicago: Rand McNally & Co., 1964) edited by Robert E. L. Faris, pp. 951–977.

C

persistent problems which has underlain each of his efforts. This is only a possible implication. But that there has been such a set of problems is, in fact, another of this study's contentions. It is incumbent upon this study, therefore, to elucidate the underlying problems, if they exist, from his major works and also the constancy of his strategy, if it too exists, as the strategy is formed in an attempt to cope with these problems. The same strategies may of course be employed to solve diverse problems, just as diverse strategies may be employed to solve the same problems. In Parsons' case, however, the nature of the problems and the nature of the strategy are fortunately made explicit in his first major work. Some part of the task of presenting support for this study's contentions is therefore made much simpler and will consist of pulling these items out from that work and arranging them economically for inspection. The next major works are not so explicit in this respect. The task then will involve greater recourse to inferential reasoning. If it can be shown that Parsons' way of articulating his materials remains logically identical to the earlier work, regardless of any differences in substance that there may be, a reasonable inference is that, although he may not believe the substance of his earlier work has completely solved the "underlying" problems, he is nevertheless of the belief that the strategy of the earlier work is essentially correct for the solution of these problems. The developmental character of Parsons' work, seen so clearly by Devereux and Williams, and occasional, unsystematic comments by Parsons in his later works, as well as references by him to his early work, shall be adduced as further support of this inference.

Before turning directly to a sketch of the problems Parsons faces, and of his method of resolving them, one final comment should be made. The questions raised and the answers that shall be developed for them in this study are directed primarily to Parsons' work. Perhaps this is enough, for any study which helped to clarify a body of work which receives so much attention and is the subject of considerable controversy would be of value. However, this emphasis should not obscure the relevance of these questions and answers to the work of others who have at times adopted formally identical strategies. Some of the work of the functionalists in particular, though not all, may be mentioned in this connection.[26] And some of the work of Parsons' critics, though again not all, has occasionally been cast in that very mode of theorizing which they criticize so severely.[27] None of this necessarily means, of course, that all who use this mode attempt to achieve the same set of objectives. But if this study can develop a clear and convincing case for the limits of this mode, of what it can and cannot do, then these limits should apply equally to anyone who adopts it. Some judgement, therefore, of how well anyone can achieve his objectives by the use of this mode may be made.

[26] *Cf.* Levy, Jr, Marion J., *The Structure of Society* (Princeton: Princeton University Press, 1952); Selznick, Philip, *Leadership in Administration* (Evanston: Row, Peterson, 1957); Aberle, D. F., Cohen, A. K., Davis, A. K., Levy, Jr., M. J. and Sutton, F. X., "The Functional Prerequisites of a Society," *Ethics*, vol. 60, 1950, pp. 100–111.

[27] There are frequent lapses in the work of A. W. Gouldner, and they appear in numerous of his essays and books. Some of these shall be referred to, when appropriate, during the text. Certain of Robert K. Merton's works may be judged similarly, and these too shall be cited upon apposite occasions in the text.

CHAPTER TWO

The First Epistemological Problems

The problem Parsons first attacks is two-fold. One part of it consists of a series of disputes over the epistemological character of various conceptions of society. The other is not directly epistemological but substantive, and is concerned with providing a scientific analysis of social action. In Parsons' early formulation the two parts of the problem are explicitly interwoven, for he believes he must overcome the various epistemological objections to the categories and concepts he wishes to use in his scientific analysis.[1] His reasoning here shall be brought out shortly. For the purposes of this study, however, it will be of the first importance to isolate the two parts and make them as clear and distinct as possible, however interwoven they may be in Parsons' conception. There are separate issues pertaining to each which cannot be appraised until they are disentangled. Each part has its own criteria of solution, and each part of the problem must be made known before a judgement may be made of the adequacy of Parsons' solutions of them.

The epistemological issues have their origin in the wide differences that exist between Parsons' conception of the standards to which scientific knowledge must conform and the standards proposed by various representatives of the historical, utilitarian and positivist traditions. Generally, it is Parsons' contention that any attempt to establish *causal relations* between the concrete facts of a society is impossible without recourse to a set of universal categories through which these facts may be ordered and related to each other. Only through the use of a set of universal categories is a general science of

[1] The interweaving of epistemological and scientific issues has been a common characteristic of much of the literature in the social sciences. Parsons amply documents this mixture in the work of many others and sets out his version of it at the very beginning. *The Structure of Social Action* (Glencoe: The Free Press, 1949, 2nd edition), see pp. 20–27.

society possible. But this is not all. Of *equal* importance is Parsons' contention that the universal categories necessary for a general science of society are to be found in more than one theoretical system. As he puts it, "... the understanding of human action involves a plurality of such theoretical systems."[2] And it is precisely this science, or understanding, that Parsons wants to achieve.

This is hardly the extent of Parsons' "epistemology"; much more of it shall be brought out later. But the presentation of these items will be enough to be able to pose the dilemmas he sees in the epistemological views of many of the historians and sociologists of the historical tradition. These views shall now be presented.

Historicism.—The dilemmas center on how society is conceived and "explained." Running through all the varieties of historicism is the conception that every society is unique, that the facts of any and all societies are fundamentally different from each other. Some of the historicists conclude that societies are not comparable, for *the conditions of existence* of any one society are unlike those of any other. But others, although agreeing that societies are unique, nevertheless attempt to find some gauge by which societies may be compared. Parsons finds none of the arguments for these views fully acceptable. What are the "conditions of existence"? And in what respects are societies unique? Let me briefly review the arguments and then present Parsons' criticisms of them.[3]

Many of the arguments, despite important differences in the elaboration of doctrines and in the development of innovations, may very roughly be grouped together. The idealistic historians may be seen to achieve an identity on the basis of certain fundamental conceptions which they hold in common. History and society, they point out, involve "man." But man, according to those who have maintained Kant's dualistic view, is to be understood both as a

[2] Parsons, *ibid.*, pp. 729–730; see also pp. 29, 294, 476, 477, 589, 704. *Cf.* "Unity and Diversity in the Modern Intellectual Disciplines: The Role of the Social Sciences," *Daedalus*, vol. 94, #1, Winter, 1965, pp. 39–65.

[3] *Cf.* Parsons' account of various of the historicist arguments, much of which I have drawn from here. *The Structure of Social Action*, chs. 13, 16, 17, 18 and 19. Other general accounts which have been helpful are Ernst Cassirer, *The Problem of Knowledge* (New Haven: Yale University Press, 1950) and *An Essay on Man* (New York: Anchor Books, 1953); see also R. G. Collingwood, *The Idea of History* (New York: Galaxy Book, 1956).

"physical object" and as a "spiritual being." As he is a physical object, man is in the phenomenal world and is thus capable of being "represented" by the natural sciences. But as he is also a spiritual being, man is not subject to physical law and is therefore "free." The study of man's spiritual aspect is the distinctive feature of the historical and cultural "sciences," for history and society characteristically involve man. Being free, man is unique; he is not a determined object in the sense of the physical sciences. Unlike "phenomena," man's spiritual being is not bound by causal law. This provides the basis for the neo-Kantian distinction between the physical and cultural sciences, with regard to their subject matter, methods, and the types of knowledge relevant to each.

All human event understood in these terms are marked by their *individuality*. If man is not bound by causal law, in what terms can his "spirit" be understood? Human life, as distinguished from mere phenomena, is "filled" with "meaning." Man's spiritual aspect can be apprehended, therefore, only by grasping the meaning of the concrete acts in which he is involved. The idealistic historicists claim that the act of knowing an age is primarily an imaginative one on the part of the historian or social scientist.[4] By an informed and sympathetic intuition, the historian reconstructs the past, gives "life" to dry documents and infuses mere artifacts with the human meaning of which they are only a clue but which they do not possess. The cardinal principle on which these doctrines rest is: "The category of meaning is not to be reduced to the category of being," but resides in a different "realm" entirely, the realm of the ideal.[5]

[4] Parsons notes that the imaginative act of knowing an age has been given the name *Verstehen* ". . . which owes more perhaps to Dilthey that to anyone else . . ." *Op. cit.*, p. 484.

[5] As Cassirer has very clearly expounded it in *An Essay on Man, op. cit.*, p. 246. Gouldner once commented, referring to a later period of Parsons' work, that Parsons' "philosophical posture (there) parallels that developed in E. Cassirer, *An Essay on Man.*" I believe the parallel to be most doubtful, for the reason that they have the most dissimilar conceptions of history. The important point to note is the *principle of irreducibility*, however, which figures so prominently in Parsons' epistemological views. See Gouldner, "Reciprocity and Autonomy in Functional Theory," *Symposium on Sociological Theory*, edited by Llewellyn Gross (Evanston: Row, Peterson, 1959), p. 257, and note 31.

The history of an age, its' "spirit," is thus identified with the constellation of meanings which was peculiar to it, and in terms of which all the events, artifacts and products occurring within it are to be understood.

Although Kant did not have as fully articulated a philosophy of history as he did of knowledge, he viewed history as a necessary development towards rationality and freedom.[6] However, the doctrine of "individuality" in the hands of certain of the idealistic historians who have retained only Kant's dualistic view has been extended so far as to conceive of each age as totally unique and unconnected to any other age. The facts of an age are ordered solely by the "spirit" of that age. History is thus an unrelated succession of "Geists."[7] Historical relativism becomes a prominent aspect of this view, for the system of meanings—the spirit—resident in each age is self-contained and has no *continuity* with the system of meanings of any other age. Each age, therefore, must be understood in-and-for itself through a sympathetic intuition. In this context, relativism is not construed merely on the basis of historical change, but on the doctrine of historical uniqueness.[8] It is maintained, therefore, that knowledge as a system of meanings cannot be properly appraised without rooting it to a given time, that "moment" of its formulation in history. Knowledge, in this sense, is relative to the age in which it was formed and cannot achieve "universal" status: there is no one set of categories, no overall meaning, that spans the immense variety of isolated constellations of meaning to be found in history.

The doctrine of the uniqueness of historical meanings, and of the extreme epistemological relativism that thereby ensues, Parsons notes, was produced as a reaction against Hegel's theory of the "laws" of the development of the world.[9] This was a reaction

[6] *Cf.* Kant's "Idea of a Universal History on a Cosmo-Political Plan," translated by Thomas De Quincey, *Speculations Literary and Philosophic* (Edinburgh: Adams and Charles Black, 1862), pp. 133–152. See also Emil L. Fackenheim's careful study, "Kant's Concept of History," *Kant-Studien*, Band 48, Heft 3, 1956/57, pp. 381–398.

[7] Parsons, *op. cit.*, p. 478; see also his *Daedalus* essay, *op. cit.*, esp. pp. 47–48.

[8] *Cf.* Maurice Mandelbaum, *The Problem of Historical Knowledge* (New York: Liveright, 1938), ch. 3, and Morris Cohen, *Reason and Nature* (Glencoe: The Free Press, 1953), ch. 1.

[9] Parsons, *The Structure of Social Action*, p. 479ff.

which, although it repudiated some of Hegel's ideas and to an extent fell back upon the dualism of Kant, mentioned previously, nevertheless also retained a few of Hegel's conceptions. There is no need to reproduce here Hegel's entire formulation of the "unfolding of the World Spirit" to make the distinctions. But a very few characteristics of his formulation should be noted, for that will make clearer two (among many) of the specific reactions against Hegel which are especially important to Parsons.

Hegel endeavored to formulate a conception in which the enormous variety in nature and culture could be incorporated and expressed in a single scheme. He conceived of history and nature as being in a process of development towards one determinate goal, namely, their ultimate unity in the *Absolute Spirit*. Different societies and various states of nature were considered, as they actually occurred in history, to be "stages" *en route* to this goal. But this does not mean that societies differ from each other merely on a quantitative basis, that is, only in terms of their "nearness to" or "farness from" the ultimate goal. The stages themselves are qualitatively distinguished from each other because of the nature of the process which produces them. For Hegel, that process is of course summed-up in the term "dialectic"—sometimes rendered in English as "sublation"—which refers to the unfolding of the Absolute Idea or *Weltgeist* out of itself by virtue of its own activity. The process consists of a continuous negating and yet retaining and transforming of everything that exists. So that, "while there is continuity in the process as a whole, each stage forms a well-marked 'system' distinct in *principle* of organization from the others and arising in direct conflict with its predecessor in the series."[10]

The part of Hegel's system that was attacked, Parsons observes, was "mainly the continuity of structural principle (the dialectic)... but the underlying mode of thinking, the attempt to organize data about the concept of a *Geist* and the unique "system" associated with it, was left undisturbed."[11] This has meant that such attempts

---

[10] Parsons, *ibid.*, p. 488 (my emphasis). A clear account of Hegel's entire system has been presented in English by W. T. Stace, *The Philosophy of Hegel* (New York: Dover Books, 1955).

[11] Parsons, *ibid.*, p. 479.

have emphasized the "organic totality" of a system of meaning, its unique, individual character, and have thus involved a repudiation of general analytical concepts. Why? Because "any attempt to break down this phenomenon (a Geist) into elements that can be subsumed under general categories of any sort destroys this individuality and leads not to valid knowledge but to a caricature of reality."[12] Of course, this does not hold for the facts of nature ("the category of being") where such facts may be, and indeed are, organized conceptually by the use of general analytical categories. "Hence," Parsons says of some in this tradition, there arose "the necessity for recognizing a source of knowledge with little place in the repertoire of science as generally understood—a kind of "intuition" for the peculiar structure of wholes which could neither be "observed" in the usual operational sense, nor constructed by the ordinary theoretical processes."[13]

Let us postpone for the moment the question whether the so-called uniqueness of any specific "Geist" indeed involves a repudiation of general analytical concepts. For a "Geist" whose scope is limited solely to one historical period is nevertheless capable of coordinating or organizing the pertinent historical data, and thus has some generality. The problem here concerns the scope of generality, and this problem will recur, much more sharply stated, in the following chapter.

There are two developments in the tradition under discussion which have served to make even more acute the dilemmas Parsons faces and attempts to overcome. One is a methodological program enunciated and carried through with such rigor that it has apparently threatened to terminate theoretical interpretation altogether. The other is a conception of judgement which impugns the "objective" character of historical knowledge and is an offshoot of the radical relativism mentioned above. Each has followed from amplifications of the philosophy of history, just sketched, by historians and sociologists who have maintained various tenets of the idealistic framework.

The prescriptions of historical particularism limit research into

---

[12] Parsons, *ibid.*, p. 480; see also p. 729.
[13] *Ibid.*, pp. 480, 481.

human events to no more than a detailing of concrete "facts."
It is the individual fact that matters, for it is of this individuality
that human life consists and in which spirit resides. But how are we
to get to the facts? Many historical and social accounts are presented
"aesthetically," that is, not only with an eye to the facts but with an
eye to the charm of their manner of presentation as well. It has even
been declared by some historians that the literal truth of their
presentation is of little importance by comparison with their success
in "portraying the spiritual stir of life."[14] For it is the spirit that one
wants ultimately to grasp. But can there be such a distinction
between life and truth? This distinction is utterly beyond comprehension. So long as we do not know the facts, any attempt to
reveal them by imposing upon them in advance our own prejudices
and principles will only distort the facts and obscure them from our
view. We must always, therefore, try to separate the personal from
the factual, to try to achieve as objective and full a presentation of
the facts as we possibly can. This "interest in the concrete detail
of historical processes for its own sake," Parsons observes, has
received ". . . perhaps its most striking methodological formulation
in Ranke's famous dictum, that the business of the historian is to
render the past *wie es eigentlich gewesen ist*, that is, in all of its
concrete detail." For it is only when we do get to the facts themselves, when we can see them as they actually are, free from any of
the deformities into which our pre-conceived notions are always in
danger of twisting them, then and only then can we come to a true
knowledge of the individuals who make up history. And it is only
through history that we can arrive, in turn, at a fullness of knowledge itself. But this conception of historical and cultural research,
Parsons remarks, ". . . has involved a repudiation of all (causal and
analytical) theory in favor of a (description) of the concrete uniqueness and individuality of all things human." The consequence has
been, Parsons believes, that " . . . methodologically . . . it can scarcely
be said to have created a school of theory in social matters—it rather
issued in a negation of theory in general." Some of the leading
figures, in addition to Ranke, are von Humboldt and Schmoller.

[14] Cassirer, *The Problem of Knowledge, op. cit.*, p. 232.

Parsons refers to them as the " 'hard boiled scientific wing of the historical school.' "[15]

However, it has been observed that the historian or social scientist does not present *all* of the facts. He cannot, for since human life is "individualistic," human acts are incapable of being subsumed and expressed either in terms of concepts or generalizations of even the narrowest scope. Scientific concepts and generalizations are abstractions whose only rightful place is in the comprehension of phenomena. "Windelband declared the judgements of natural science to be nomethetic, those of history to be idiographic. The former give us general laws; the latter describe particular facts."[16] Human life is of such richness, and so diverse in its manifold individuality, that no description of life can ever be fully exhaustive. The historian or social scientist can only describe human life in terms of *quality*, for this is the characteristic of individuality which in fact admits of no degrees. The description of life is therefore always selective. In actual research, specific facts are brought together to make a meaningful whole. There must, therefore, be some selective *principle* at work. It is held that the very selection and synthesis of facts is directed by the historian's and sociologist's own interests, volitions and values.[17] All of the descriptions they offer us, no matter how carefully authenticated or how far-ranging, are "affected" by their values. To the extent that this obtains, even the meaning which a historian "intuits," regardless of how great his empathetic powers

[15] Parsons, *op. cit.*, p. 477. There have been similar interpretations of Ranke's views; see Benedetto Croce, *Theory and History of Historiography*, trans. by Douglas Ainslie (London: Harrap, 1921), p. 292ff. There are also opposed interpretations; see Cassirer, *op. cit.*, ch. XIII and conclusion.

[16] Cassirer, *An Essay on Man*, p. 235; *cf.* Parsons, *Daedalus, op. cit.*, and *The Structure of Social Action*, p. 476.

[17] The affective, volitional, valuational, etc. characteristics of "the knower" have been propounded and emphasized by Wilhelm Dilthey—but with no intention of raising skeptical issues. He rather intended by this to form a bridge to the historical—spiritual—world. A brief review of some of his ideas is to be found in Mandelbaum, *op. cit.*, pp. 58–67. Some of Dilthey's writings have been translated into English. See *Wilhelm Dilthey: Selected Readings From His Works and an Introduction to His Sociological and Philosophic Work*, by H. A. Hodges (London: Routledge and Kegan Paul, 1951); and also *Wilhelm Dilthey: Pattern and Meaning in History, Thoughts on History and Society*, edited by H. P. Dickman (New York: Harper Torchbooks, 1962).

for past meanings may be, is bound to be affected by the values and desires he holds. That which is meaningful, in fact, is meaningful in terms of his own interests, desires and values. Whether the interests, etc., are his own or the age in which he lives is of no consequence. In either case, his presentation of the facts is not dictated by the existence of the facts alone but by factors which limit his selection and apprehension of them. When knowledge is seen to be "value-charged," an extreme form of subjectivism is coupled to the relativism mentioned previously. Knowledge, particularly of human life, can be neither objective nor universal. All of the assertions, therefore, made by historians or social scientists located in different settings or in different "ages," so long as they are "charged" with different values and desires, are truly *incomparable*. Since this view was put forth, Parsons comments, "the same tendency has been carried still further onto the epistemological plane by the . . . movement known as *Wissensoziologie*."[18]

It will be useful at this point to highlight summarily the differences that have been construed to exist between the types of knowledge relevant to the natural and social disciplines.

Knowledge of the phenomenal world, the world of interest to the natural sciences, is abstract, conceptual and analytical. Such knowledge is arranged formally in a systematic theory. In the sense of regularity and law, the phenomenal world is determined: "causality" is a fundamental category. In the sense of analysis and conceptual theory, knowledge of the phenomenal world is fundamentally rational. Knowledge of phenomena is presumed to be "value free" and thus "supra temporal" and, in this respect, is understood to be not relative but universal. Since the only development that was held to occur in the natural sciences is one of accretion, knowledge of phenomena was believed to grow quantitatively, progressing on the "same" foundations, and hence to be essentially "static." "Objectivity" is thus understood in terms of "formal criteria" of detachment.

Since human life, on the other hand, is "free," it cannot be apprehended by abstractions or regularities. Human life is concrete

---

[18] *Op. cit.*, p. 480. *Cf.* Karl Mannheim, *Ideology and Utopia* (New York: Harcourt, Brace & Co., 1949) esp. pp. 168, 211, 238, 261, 263.

and particular and is intuitively grasped as, and expressed through, an "image." In the sense of freedom from law, human life is indetermined: "meaning" is a fundamental category. In the sense of intuition and image (as opposed to analysis and concept) knowledge of human life is fundamentally "irrational." Knowledge is value-charged and thus highly temporal and is understood, therefore, to be relative. Since there can be no development within the cultural sciences, knowledge of human life is organic rather than progressive; it does not grow by accretion but shows discontinuous, logically unrelated shifts with each of the unique constellations of meaning which is apprehended. Hence the knowledge gathered by the cultural sciences is essentially changing and dynamic. "Objectivity" is considered to be a matter of the objects perceived and, in addition to material evidence, is held to consist of the historian's or sociologist's stance and participation in human life and is thus variable without limit.[19]

All of the items presented in this dichotomous version of knowledge are by no means adhered to by every historicist who accepts the dualism postulated by Kant. Nevertheless, one or another of them has been stressed by Neo-Kantian scholars, and together they constitute the problems Parsons attempts to overcome.

The Epistemological Problems of the Historical Standpoint.— Confronted with Parsons' first requirement, that universal categories are necessary to establish causal relations between concrete facts, the entire historical standpoint reviewed must be seen to lead to a disasterous outcome, namely, epistemological skepticism. It is not possible from that standpoint to establish causal relations between facts. They can merely be observed and described and placed in temporal sequence—as in fact Ranke, among others, urged that they should be. But this is no more, as Parsons sees it, than the "methodological counterpart of Hume's skepticism in epistemology."[20] No comprehension of how facts are related to each other may be had. No connection between facts other than the perceptual one of observing them take place conjointly or at different points in time can be made. Treated in this fashion, facts—whether of

---

[19] *Cf.* Karl Mannheim's essay, "Historicism," in *Essays on the Sociology of Knowledge* (New York: Oxford University Press, 1952).

[20] Parsons, *op. cit.*, p. 729.

individual events or of individual constellations of meaning—are a mere accumulation of details, an aggregate with no inner order. And by whatever other terms such an aggregate may be characterized, it may not be called scientific knowledge. Parsons finds this cognitively unacceptable. One of the tasks he sets himself is to establish the *possibility* of achieving a general science of society. By showing that it is possible to make causal statements of the facts of society, and thus relate facts to each other, he can overcome the skeptical consequences of the historical view. Notice that this *also* means he can overturn the extreme relativism that follows from the views, so briefly touched on before, of Dilthey and Windelband, For if Parsons can indeed provide a set of *universal* categories by which the facts of society may be causally related to each other, then he will have paved the way to showing how *societies* may be compared, and the conception of idiographic judgements as the one and only permissable mode of judging the facts of societies will collapse. Nor is this all, for if Parsons can show that *the* set of universal categories he provides must *always* be used when describing or thinking of certain facts of society, then he can, at the same time, show how *assertions* of society may be compared. And once it can be shown how assertions may be compared, the doctrine of their *extreme* subjectivism will be undermined and will also collapse.[21]

Parsons is thus led to an epistemological examination of "facts." Part of his analysis attempts to show that the description of even the most unique of the facts of any society logically requires the presuppostion of more general terms, that is, of some conceptual scheme. And even when this requirement is unrecognized, or is ruled out as a matter of principle, as is presumably the case with Ranke, the conceptual scheme is nevertheless tacitly presupposed. "It is fundamental," says Parsons in the *Introduction* to his first major work, "that there is no empirical knowledge which is not in some sense and to some degree conceptually formed ... description of the facts involves a conceptual scheme ... "[22]

But what is a "fact" itself? "A fact," says Parsons, "is understood to be an "empirically verifiable statement about phenomena in

21 *Ibid.*, pp. 732ff.
22 *Ibid.*, p. 28.

terms of a conceptual scheme' . . . a fact is not itself a phenomenon at all, but a proposition *about* one or more phenomena."[23] It follows, then, that a "system of scientific theory is generally abstract precisely because the facts it embodies do *not* constitute a complete description of the concrete phenomena involved . . . (but only those characteristics of) the phenomena which are important to the theoretical system that is being employed at the time."[24]

Once Parsons has made these points he must then do two things: (1) identify the characteristics of the phenomena of interest to him, and (2) provide a clear statement of the conceptual scheme which allowed him to select the particular characteristics that he did. Not until such a scheme is explicitly stated can the manifold of social characteristics be brought under intellectual control. It is precisely at this juncture that the second of Parsons' "epistemological requirements" *also* comes to the fore, namely, that the understanding of human action involves a plurality of theoretical systems. The first of his requirements may be said to raise the question: how is knowledge of society possible? The second is no longer concerned merely with showing the possibility of knowledge but of specifying its necessary constituents. That is, Parsons must now show that certain definite and identifiable "theoretical systems" are each necessary fully to organize the characteristics of the phenomena of his interest. These systems are to be found in the idealistic, utilitarian and positivist traditions, as Parsons calls them. But there is a difficult problem here, for each of the "necessary" systems is "imperialistic"—that is, claims are made of each which rule out the claims made of the others. Parsons, therefore, is also led into a critical examination of these claims. The idealistic historicists, it will be recalled, claimed that "the category of meaning is not to be reduced to the category of being," and they then tended to assimilate all human actions into the category of "meaning." "Indeed," Parsons has again said some thirty years after his first analysis, they "carried this emphasis to an extreme comparable in certain respects to the extremism of physical *reductionism*."[25] They thus denied "the possibility or

---

[23] *Ibid.*, p. 41.
[24] *Ibid.*, p. 41 (my emendation).
[25] *Daedalus, op. cit.*, p. 49 (my emphasis).

validity of general concepts in the field of human action."[26] However, in making these claims, the idealistic historicists conspicuously failed "to consider clearly how the 'realms' (or categories) interacted with each other."[27] Some members of the positivist tradition, on the other hand, claim "that the concrete phenomena to which (their general) theory is applicable are ... exclusively understandable in terms of the categories of (their) system." Behaviorism, as Parsons notes, also carries "through the common tendency of the reduction of the factors of human behavior to biological terms." But these extreme claims for the positivist disciplines, Parsons, argues, involve the commitment of the fallacy of 'misplaced concreteness.' Thus physical reductionism would be, in Whitehead's terms, "merely the accidental error of mistaking the abstract for the concrete ... (which) I will call the 'Fallacy of Misplaced Concreteness.' "[28] Physical reductionism is indeed "... correct in insisting on the scientific legitimacy of general theoretical concepts," Parsons allows, but it is "wrong in its interpretation of their status to concrete reality. There can be no doubt of the applicability of the systems of the physical sciences to human action, but attempts to exhaust ... explanation (of human action) in such terms have broken down."[29]

The usual way of resolving the incompatibility of the claims made by the adherents of "the two patterns of extremism, physical reductionism and historical uniqueness," Parsons observes, has been "to keep the fields of their application rigidly distinct, as is done in the (idealistic) distinction between the natural and the socio-cultural sciences."[30] "It will not, however, do," he says, "merely to say that both the positivistic and the idealistic positions have certain justifications and there is a sphere in which each should be recognized. It is necessary, rather, to go beyond such eclecticism, to attempt, at least in outline, an account of the specific modes of interrelationship

[26] Parsons, *The Structure of Social Action, op. cit.,* p. 715.

[27] Parsons, *Daedalus, op. cit.,* p. 47.

[28] Parsons, *The Structure of Social Action,* pp. 117, 728, 730; Whitehead, Alfred North, *Science and The Modern World* (New York: Mentor Books, 1949, 2nd printing), pp. 52 and 57.

[29] Parsons, *ibid.,* 729.

[30] *Ibid.,* p. 476; see also *Daedalus, op. cit.,* p. 49.

between the two."[31] But can the positions be divested of the dogmatic, apparently irreconcilable, claims that many of their proponents have imposed upon them? Parsons believes they can if the modes of their interrelations are carefully enough specified. Let us turn now very briefly to examine the main features of the program Parsons follows in attempting to interrelate the various intellectual disciplines of his concern. Then we shall look, again very briefly, at the positivist and utilitarian viewpoints, and this chapter may be brought to a conclusion with a restatement of the problem.

The Analytical Program.—So long as we remain at the level of phenomena we can never escape from their variety and diversity. But every phenomenon is actually a complex event. One way to bring the phenomenal world under rational control is to break these complex events into their elements, to seek to find, within the phenomena themselves, the components which make them up. The analysis of an event splits the event into its component parts. Once we have these parts we are then able to reproduce the event and, by so doing, reveal its structure, for not only is the event reproduced in its totality but in the *ordered sequence* of its elements. Phenomena, then, are the starting point. The main trouble with the historicists is that this was just the place at which they stopped, for they believed "phenomena" to be, in the older logical language, a *"terminus a quo"*—a point from which knowledge proceeds merely by the aggregation of more and more "phenomena." But further observation of phenomena will give us simply more phenomena. By analysis and not merely repeated observations can we master phenomena and transform their coexistence into a "determinate" existence. Analysis enables us to find the principles—the conditions and presuppositions —of their occurrence. Here, then, is at least a clue of the way to be taken to avoid the epistemological skepticism of the historicists' views: by showing that the phenomena to which they refer are subject to analysis. Those "phenomena" are the various "descriptions" of the Geist that have already been encountered.

When the occurrence of an event has been analyzed into the complex of causes and effects which produced it, the event itself may be seen as a "system." An event, in other words, is not made up

[31] Parsons, *The Structure of Social Action*, p. 486.

D

simply of so many parts which can be summed. Its parts hang together and give it structure. Thus, although the identification of these parts is of the first importance, merely tallying them will not reproduce the event. Every event analyzed depicts a "whole" which is constituted of its parts and their relations. To reveal the structure of an event is the complete aim of analysis. To anticipate: the problem with the historicist conception, then, is that it identifies only one of the parts of the event of interest to Parsons, that event being: social action. As Devereux so well puts it: "Ideas were treated as altogether too free, and hence essentially free floating."[32] Ideas have to be treated as a part of a system which contains yet other parts, and the relationships among them have to be specified.

At the root of the analytical approach, then, are four major assumptions: (1) that phenomena are the data of science; (2) but that phenomena do not exist as a mere jumble of incomprehensible data—they are governed by and may be grounded in some set of universal categories and rules which it is the task of analysis to discern; (3) that these universal categories and rules are no less real because they cannot be observed—they are actually constitutive of the event, they are its parts and their relations, and without them the event would not be possible; (4) that the constituents of an event form a system the complete elucidation of which is the final goal of analysis. This is the general program Parsons adheres to and he has stated it explicitly and in detail throughout his first major work.[33] Indeed, the program is based upon an anologue to Newton's methods. But perhaps I have stated the program too succinctly and a brief, simple example would be useful to illustrate the program's ingredients.

In discussing how Newton based his own procedure upon Galileo's, Ernst Cassirer remarks that:[34]

The path of a projectile could not be described directly from observation; it could not simply be abstracted from a great number of observations. Observation gives us to be sure certain general characteristics; it shows us

[32] *The Social Theories of Talcott Parsons*, cited in ch. I, p. 18.
[33] Parsons, *op. cit.*, chs. I, II, XVI, XIX.
[34] *The Philosophy of the Enlightenment* (Boston: Beacon Press, 1955), pp. 10–11.

that a phase of ascent is followed by a phase of descent, etc. But observation fails to produce any precise determination of the path of a projectile. We arrive at a truly mathematical conception of an event by tracing the phenomenon back to its peculiar conditions, by isolating each set of conditions simultaneously affecting the event, and by investigating these sets of conditions with respect to their laws. The law of the parabolic path of the projectile may be found, and the increase and decrease of velocity may be exactly recorded once the phenomenon of projection has been shown to be a complex event, the determination of which depends on two different forces, that of the original impulse and that of gravity.

Despite its success in comprehending phenomena, analysis never truly ends. It must begin again at every new stage of empirical science. Every set of principles (categories and rules) is true and useful only to the extent that it adequately comprehends a given range of phenomena. A set of principles describes and orders phenomena. But future observations and further analysis may allow for even more adequate principles of the phenomena to be found. Analytical categories and rules are therefore provisional; they are geared to a particular body of observations and they must be constructed anew at least with every change in our observations.

The historicists have provided Parsons with one, highly unstable, "part" of that system he is interested in: social action. A very few words shall now be said of the other parts contributed by the utilitarian and positivist traditions.

The Utilitarian and Positivist Contributions.—Utilitarian thought, as Parsons conceives it, has been concerned with the place of rationality in human action. "Historically," he says, "this concept of rationality of action, not always clearly and unambiguously stated, has played the central role in . . . the utilitarian branch of the positivistic tradition."[35] The utilitarian schemes define human action as rational when means are selected to achieve a particular end. This definition gives to human action a voluntary aspect, for human beings are thus conceived as choosing beings. And if human beings are choosing beings, they are individuals. But if they are individuals,

[35] Parsons, *op. cit.*, p. 699.

this means that human beings have no ends, as it were, in common. Each individual carries out his separate acts, he chooses the most efficient means available to him to pursue his idiosyncratic end. "The rational unit act which has been described," observes Parsons, is considered to be a "concrete unit of concrete systems of action . . . (and) by assuming that a concrete system as a whole is made up only of units of this character we get the picture of a complete concrete system of rational action."[36] Parsons characterizes utilitarian thought as emphasizing the following four features: "atomism (stress on the individual act), rationality (stress on the choice of efficient means), empiricism (stress on the concreteness, the 'reality,' of individual acts), and randomness of ends (stress on the uncommon, idiosyncratic nature of the goals men pursue)."[37]

The conceptual dilemma that follows from this characterization of human action may be put in the form of a question: if the ends of individual human beings vary at random, what is it that holds society together?[38] That every society is held together in some way, that the social activities of human beings exhibit some pattern, that social life is not utterly chaotic—these are not mere chimeras but data of observation. Can they be understood on a utilitarian basis alone? The explanation of such data constitutes the *problem* of social order. To understand the general principles of the 'determinateness' of social life is of central concern in all Parsons' thought, and is in fact a conceptual, not a political, concern. A political concern would be expressed, *possibly*, by formulating the particular principles of a distinctive pattern of social activity. In any case, the various utilitarian solutions to the general problem shall hardly be examined here. It is sufficient to note them and to note also that Parsons finds them unacceptable. It was Hobbes, in Parsons' account, who gave the problem its classic statement. In deducing "the character of the concrete system which would result if its units were in fact as defined," Hobbes observed that "men will adopt to (their) immediate end the most efficient means . . . force and fraud. This is nothing but a state of war." And in a state of war the immediate and disparate

---

[36] Parsons, *op. cit.*, p. 59.
[37] Parsons, *op. cit.*, p. 60 (my parenthetical additions).
[38] *Ibid.*, pp. 64, 67.

ends of all men are placed in the greatest jeopardy. Hence, in the interests of their self-preservation it is necessary that there be a controlling agency over men, that men will give over to a sovereign power a monopoly on the use of force. But "this solution," argues Parsons, "really involves stretching, at a critical point, the conception of rationality beyond its scope in the rest of the theory, to a point where actors come to realize the situation as a whole instead of pursuing their own ends in terms of their immediate situations . . ."[39] And this solution yet further violates Hobbes' own premise, that men pursue only their own immediate and hence *random* ends, for Hobbes' ". . . way of accounting for the origin of the sovereign is . . . to posit a momentary identity—in security—from which the social contract is derived."[40] Locke's solution of the problem was able to escape the contradictions in which Parsons believes Hobbes' argument became involved only by the use of what Parsons dubs an extra-scientific, metaphysical prop, namely, the postulation of a "natural identity of interests." However, this postulate from which ordered action may be deduced solely by recourse to an ever greater number of *ad hoc* assumptions, Parsons argues, is scientifically indefensible.[41]

"The basic question," Parsons states again three decades after his original analysis of these matters, "is why, having freedom of choice, people in fact opt for one, not some other, personal goal and means of attaining it."[42] The utilitarian framework is simply too narrow for the larger theoretical task, of explaining social order generally. That which remains valuable in utilitarian thought, Parsons concludes in his early work, is the statement of the problem, especially in Hobbes' formulation of it, and the stress utilitarianism places upon the voluntary aspect of human action. It is this stress that makes human action meaningful. Utilitarian thought, then, has provided two "categories"—means and ends—which, when properly grounded and reformulated, may be of service in a general theory of social action.

[39] *Ibid.*, pp. 90, 93, 283.
[40] *Ibid.*, p. 283 (my emphasis).
[41] *Ibid.*, pp. 96, 102, 701.
[42] *Ibid.*, pp. 491–492; the quotation is from the *Daedalus* essay, *op. cit.*, p. 53.

There developed two other lines of thought on "the problem of social order" which diverged sharply from some of the utilitarian premises sketched. Parsons characterizes each as being positivistic. One he calls "radical rationalistic positivism," the other "radical anti-intellectualistic positivism." The first erases "the distinctions between ends, means and conditions of rational action, making action a process only of adaptation to given conditions and predictions of their future state."[43] The adaptation of men to given conditions will then be a function of how much they do or do not know of these conditions. The more men know, the more rational will be their behavior; the less men know, the less rational. "Irrationality" of behavior is then simply a product of ignorance and error. That which a human being chooses to pursue is presumed to be based "on (his) scientific knowledge of some empirical reality." But to think of a human being's ends or goals to be merely a function of the state of his knowledge, of what he knows or does not know, has "had the inevitable logical consequence of assimilating ends to the situation of action and destroying their independence ... For the only possible basis of empirical knowledge of a future state of affairs is prediction on the basis of knowledge of present and past states. Then action becomes determined *entirely* by its conditions," Parsons observes, "for without the independence of ends the distinction between conditions and means becomes meaningless."[44] Once the independence of ends as a factor in human action is denied, Parsons points out, the door is opened for the further "assimilation (of ends) to the conditions of the situation, that is, to elements analyzable in terms of nonsubjective categories, principally heredity and environment." The anti-intellectualistic positivists then would explain human behavior as a function of instincts, drives, reinforcement, the pleasure principle, and the like. However, to speak of pleasure, for example, as a goal or end of behavior, argues Parsons, "has nothing to do with the analytical concept of end as part of a generalized system. (The pleasure principle) is a feature of the organism which we know by experience we can count on to

[43] *The Structure of Social Action*, p. 699.
[44] *Ibid*., pp. 63–64.

operate in certain ways, and which hence belongs analytically to the conditions of action."[45]

Positivistic thought organizes our information of the conditions in which human action takes place. The positivists tell us, therefore, of the constraints that are "always" placed upon human action. But how are we to assess the limits of positivistic thought, how are we to qualify that category—"conditions"—which allows us to understand a part of human action? "It must not be forgotten," says Parsons, "that there may well be hereditary elements which 'drive' behavior in conformity (say) with a rational norm ... (and) ... insofar as this is true, whatever subjective aspect there is to action will turn out, on thorough investigation, to be reducible to terms of non-subjective systems. The test is *always* whether an *adequate* explanation of the concrete behavior in question can be attained without reference to the elements formulated in concepts with an inherent subjective reference."[46] But that is precisely the test of each of the concepts Parsons wishes to employ. The general questions Parsons attempts to answer, at least in his first work, may now be stated more intelligibly.

The Problems.—Parsons is attempting, in his first major work, to lay the ground for a *general* solution of the problem of social order. In this attempt, he reviews a number of solutions that have been given by other investigators of the problem. The historicist solutions, as has been seen, are no general solution at all. The historicists, in fact, would deny to Parsons' attempt "any legitimacy as a scientific aim," as Parsons himself is well aware.[47] Indeed, the historicists would consider the problem as stated to be well-nigh meaningless, for they would tend to rule out on "metaphysical" grounds even the *possibility* of a general solution to the problem of social order, a general theory of the manifold patternings of social life. Their own views of the nature of society, and of the nature of the judgements that are made of societies, must lead to an epistemological skepticism when brought up against the standard of generality by which Parsons wishes to judge a solution of the problem. The utilitarians,

[45] *Ibid.*, pp. 64, 700.   [46] *Ibid.*, p. 701 (my emphasis).   [47] *Ibid.*, p. 729.

on the other hand, in their attempt to present a general solution of the problem of social order are led either into a violating of their own first premises, or into a postulating of metaphysical assumptions. Their solutions are either contradictory or not justifiable on scientific grounds. The utilitarians, therefore, although they have been able to perceive the problem with some clarity, have failed in their attempts to solve the problem. The positivists, finally, in keeping with their own premises, believe that human behavior is, as Parsons has phrased the belief, "determined entirely by its conditions." And the conditions in which human life exists are physical, biological, chemical, physiological, and so on. The positivists are thus led to assume that all of human life may be explained by the conceptual schemes of the physical sciences. Sociology as a "separate science," on their assumption, would therefore tend to evaporate. But until all of human behavior is explained by the conceptual systems of the physical sciences, the assumption that it all *can* be so explained must be judged as gratuitous.

Each of the attempts Parsons has reviewed has been successful at "solving" a part of the general problem, but no one of them has, by itself, been able to solve the entire general problem. Parsons is thus brought to the conclusion that a general solution of the problem of social order will require a plurality of theoretical schemes. But since the solution must be a general one, each scheme must be analytical in its own right *and be interrelated* with the others as well. If the schemes are not interrelated in some consistent way with each other, the solution will fail to be general—it will be merely eclectic, and the orders of phenomena to which each scheme refers will remain indeterminate with respect to each other. And if sociology is to be one of the theoretical schemes that is used, it too must be shown to be analytical. The schemes, therefore, cannot simply be taken together: interrelating them and showing that sociology is "analytical" will require a different scheme altogether.

Parsons, then, has three major problems: (1) he must show that a general solution of the problem of social order is possible; (2) he must show that social order, as he conceives it, cannot be explained generally without using a plurality of theoretical systems, each analytical and each interrelated with the others; and (3) he must show that his solution does provide, in fact, an explanation of social order. Notice that the first two problems, which are here called epistemological, cannot be solved in any detail until the third, substantive problem is solved. They are epistemological, that is, for they raise questions of the characteristics of knowledge. And in this case they may be taken to raise questions which will make clear the exact categories, and their interrelations, that are "found" in the general explanation given of the problem of social order. The explanation itself, therefore, must precede any clear answers that may be given to the epistemological questions.

It is not difficult to show that the apprehension of the most unique of events will require the conceptual use of at least one logical universal of some sort. That this is a conceptual requirement of thought has, in fact, often been shown; and it has even been argued by those in close sympathy to the historical school that Windelband's conception of "idiographic judgements" cannot be upheld.[48] But to say that we must use logical universals in our thinking is not equivalent to saying *which* logical universals we must use. Once a scientific explanation of some event has been given, one of the epistemological problems may then become: what are the conceptual presuppositions necessary for this explanation? The epistemological analysis will proceed until a conclusion of this sort may be stated: without such and such presuppositions (that is, the "logical universals" that have now been clearly identified) this particular explanation could not have been made. In this version of epistemological analysis, the epistemological aim is to establish exactly the categories that are necessarily employed in the explanation at hand, and without which the explanation could not have been forthcoming. But to be able to say that certain, definite categories are necessarily used in *this* explanation clearly depends for its saying on first having, and then examining, the explanation itself. I must insist on this point, not only because I believe it correct, but for the reason that it will be seen to shed a certain critical light on Parsons' thinking.

Having reviewed the problems that Parsons sees in the historicist,

[48] *Cf.* Morris Cohen, *op. cit.*, also Cassirer, *Essay on Man*, *op. cit.*, pp. 222–223, 236.

utilitarian and positivist traditions, it may more readily be understood that there is a dual set of interests in his work, epistemological and scientific. Parsons sets out simultaneously to establish the *possibility* of sociological knowledge, with some conception of the features such knowledge should possess, as well as to give us that knowledge itself. But why, it may be asked, does Parsons concern himself with the epistemological problems at all? Why not simply get on with the explanation and give us that knowledge he believes the historicists, utilitarians and positivists do not give us? It should be recalled that a solution of the epistemological problem is precisely that which will give to Parsons' scientific concern, at least as he understands it, its legitimacy as a scientific aim. "The whole purpose of this study," he says of his early work, "... is to work out the outline of just such a system of general theoretical categories, having demonstrable empirical validity."[49] Solving the epistemological problems, then, will also serve to neutralize the competing claims made by various adherents of the traditions reviewed. However, from the argument of the preceding paragraphs it would follow that Parsons' epistemological intentions cannot be carried out *fully* until his scientific aim has been achieved. For only upon that achievement can the voicing of historicist, utilitarian and positivist claims be —logically—stilled.

Therefore, in judging Parsons' work we must first of all be able to tell when his scientific aim has in fact been achieved. We must have, that is, some standards by which we may gauge the adequacy of the explanation Parsons gives. Parsons himself refers to one such standard, and it has been encountered at various points throughout this chapter, namely, when he speaks of the establishment of causal relationships between the concrete facts of a society. His view that a causal relationship between facts cannot be established without recourse to a set of general categories (or "universals" in the logical sense) is indeed congruent with the "covering law" model of scientific explanation. Thus Parsons endorses the commonly held Aristotelian conception of the enthymematic character of scientific thought, as shall be seen clearly in the discussion of the following chapter. Perhaps this endorsement will give his scientific critics

[49] Parsons, *op. cit.*, p. 729.

some pause, although it is not at issue here and will not be explored.[50] In any event, what follows from Parsons' view is simply this: that in a *causal* explanation at least *some* of the propositions of a scientific theory must take the logical form, "if p, then q"—where "q" stands for the concrete behavior to be explained, "p" stands for some set of concrete conditions, and taken together the expression may be read: "whenever p occurs, q occurs." This may be a weak condition to which a causal explanation should conform, but the explanation must nevertheless conform to it. A causal explanation of the "if p, then q" sort cannot possibly be given unless there is some system of general categories from which this explanation may be deduced. The lack of such a system and the consequent inability to provide a causal explanation, it will be recalled, is the nub of Parsons' criticism of the historicist views.

Parsons makes a number of comments throughout his first work which may be taken to signify agreement as to the (minimal) logical form a causal proposition should take. Some of these comments shall now quickly be noted before turning, in the next chapters, to Parsons' solution of the problems that have been set out. (1) "For the purpose of explanation," Parsons says, it is necessary to generalize "the conceptual scheme so as to bring out the functional relations involved in the facts already descriptively arranged."[51] This necessity, we may infer, will allow a statement of the "if p, then q" sort to be made, where "p" and "q" respectively refer to different sets of facts and "if" and "then" refer to their functional relations. (2) "Theory proper," Parsons states, ". . . is confined to the formulation and logical relations of propositions containing empirical facts in direct relation to the observations of the facts and thus empirical verification of the propositions."[52] (3) "A theoretical system," Parsons says, "does not merely state facts which have been observed and their logically deducible relations to other facts which have also

---

[50] *Cf.* R. B. Braithwaite, *Scientific Explanation* (New York: Harper Torchbooks, 1960); also Carl G. Hempel and Paul Oppenheim, "The Logic of Explanation," in *Readings in the Philosophy of Science* edited by Herbert Feigl and May Brodbeck (New York: Appleton-Crofts, Inc., 1953), pp. 319–352.

[51] Parsons, *op. cit.*, p. 49.

[52] *Ibid.*, p. 24.

been observed. In so far as such a theory is empirically correct it will also tell us what empirical facts it should be possible to observe in a given set of circumstances."[53] Points (2) and (3) taken together may be restated as follows: *vindication* of a theory will consist of ascertaining whether the empirical relations we are led by deduction to believe to hold, in fact do hold. Finally, (4) in elucidating the meaning of the term "system," Parsons states: "... 'system' has been employed throughout in two different senses which should be made clear. On the one hand, it refers to a body of *logically* interrelated propositions, a 'theoretical system'; on the other, to a body of interrelated phenomena, an empirical system. The first kind of system is not only not a 'real' system at all, it does not state any facts in the ordinary sense. It merely defines general properties of empirical phenomena and states general relations between their values. In applying the theoretical system to empirical phenomena, data, ordinarily called facts, must be supplied. These data constitute the specific 'values' of the general categories which make up the system of theory. If, of course, the empirically given values of one or more variables are known, other facts can be ascertained about the same empirical system, by applying the theory."[54] A theory, then, must always be *interpreted* for there to be any application of the theory to empirical phenomena. Lacking an interpretation that would allow us to ascertain any of the values of the general categories that make up the system of theory, the theory would remain unvindicated.

In some part, the frequent allegation of an a-historical outlook to Parsons' thought may be settled here:[55] if, in fact, it can be shown that his work will not admit of an interpretation which would distinguish the values of the immensely broad "scale" of the concrete facts of action pertinent to different societies at different historical times, his work may be judged unvindicated and a-historical as well.

[53] *Ibid.*, p. 8.
[54] *Ibid.*, p. 71.
[55] *Cf.* Robert A. Nisbet, *Social Change and History* (New York: Oxford University Press, 1968), ch. 8.

CHAPTER THREE

The Relativity of Ideal-Types

Perhaps it would be expected from the concluding comments of the previous chapter that in his first major work Parsons would embark upon the construction of a scientific theory from which a number of causal propositions could be deduced. And in a sense this is what he does, although it is a sense, not perfectly obvious, and the purpose of this and following chapter will be to try make that sense as clear as possible. In his first work Parsons is concerned mainly with showing that such a theory is in fact already present, at least implicitly, in the diverse works of Alfred Marshall, Vilfredo Pareto, Emile Durkheim and Max Weber.[1] Parsons' intention is to show that the separate works of each of these men converge upon a single system of general categories, and that the various explanations of social events each man gives are actually grounded in this single set of categories. To establish the definition of these categories, and that the categories in question are necessarily presupposed in the works that he considers, are epistemological pursuits, as defined previously. It is of no concern to this study to ask, for example, whether Parsons has successfully demonstrated such convergence, or whether the set of categories he claims are presupposed in the works of the aforementioned writers are indeed presupposed. For the sake of following Parsons' line of argument, his claims will be dealt with as though established, and I shall note the consequences that follow from these claims. They may for the moment be summarized by saying again that Parsons has attempted to lay the ground for the determinate analysis of all social facts in a *universal* fashion. To see this clearly, it will be useful to examine, if even briefly, Parsons' critique of Max Weber's approach to the analysis of social facts.

[1] Parsons, *The Structure of Social Action*, ch. 1.

It may be recalled that one of the distinctive characteristics of Weber's approach to factual materials is his use of "ideal types." At what point do such types enter in the analysis of facts? Parsons makes clear that Weber, first of all, is in agreement with the historical school that the values of the sociologist or historian make him sensitive to certain problems and guide his expression of them. Values, in this respect, are "relevant" to the problems in which the social scientist has an interest. But once the problem is construed, Weber maintains, it is the problem, not the scientist's values, which directs his observations. Weber thus draws a distinction between the social scientist as a valuing subject, and the independence of the social scientist's observations. The problems which the social scientist formulates are a "function" of his values, whereas his observations are a "function" of the problem. From this, the validity of the social scientist's results is not to be challenged on subjectivistic grounds.[2] At worst, there is a relativity of problems. What the social scientist has established on the basis of his observations, however, remains "valid" even though the interest in certain problems varies from one age to the next, or from one social scientist to another.[3] The social scientist is thus not at all "value free," in the sense that he is disembodied, de-spiritualized, or without interests.

It is important to emphasize that for Weber—and for Heinrich Rickert as well, to whom Weber gives explicit acknowledgement for the first formulation of this idea[4]—"value-relevance" is conceived to apply only to the social sciences. The natural sciences are presumed to be unified by only one interest in their subject matter, namely, "control of phenomena." This single interest is defined as the ". . . building of systems of general theory verifiable in terms of and applicable to a wide range of concrete phenomena . . . (where) . . . the individual phenomenon is a 'case'."[5] The social sciences, however,

---

[2] *Ibid.*, p. 594.

[3] *Ibid.*, p. 600.

[4] See Rickert, *Die Grenzen der naturwissenschaftlichen Begriffsbildung* (Tübingen, 1929, 5th edition), ch. IV, sec. 2; see Weber, *The Methodology of the Social Sciences* (Glencoe: The Free Press, 1949), trans. H. A. Finch and E. A. Shils, pp. 148–150; *cf.* Mandelbaum's discussion of Rickert, cited in ch. 2, pp. 119–147.

[5] Parsons, *op. cit.*, pp. 592–598.

are marked by the diversity of the *objects* of their interest, namely individual and particular events, as well as the *diverse* nature of their interests. Thus, the problem arises: given the particularity of objects and interests of concern to social scientists, "how is it possible to prove the existence of a causal relation between certain features of a given historical individual and certain empirical facts which have existed prior to it?"[6] Parsons' analysis of Weber's procedure in dealing with this problem is as follows:

First, the historical individual—or the object of causal analysis, the thing to be explained—must be simplified. Whether the individual is the Indian caste system, modern rational bourgeois capitalism, Chinese patrimonial bureaucracy—whatever it is, "it must be reduced to what is essential, omitting the unimportant. Thus in Indian caste, for example, the complex details of the hierarchical aspect of caste structure are disregarded and only the fact of hierarchical relation to the Brahmins is kept in view. But though simplified, and in the sense involved in value-relevance one-sided, such a concept is still definitely *individual*; there is one and only one Indian caste system. The construction of such historical individuals has the function of preparing and organizing the concrete material for causal analysis."[7] Such individuals are one kind of ideal-type. But explanation requires that another kind of "ideal-type" be used, a kind that involves general concepts.

"The causal explanation of an individual event requires an answer to the question what would, under certain hypothetical, hence unreal but nevertheless 'possible' assumptions, have happened!" A general ideal-type, Parsons says, "is such a construction of a hypothetical course of events with two other characteristics: (1) abstract generality and (2) the ideal-typical exaggeration of empirical reality. Without the first ... the concept might be applicable only to a single historical individual; without the second it might be merely a common trait or a statistical average. It is neither of these, but is an ideal construction of a *typical* course of action, or form of relationship which is applicable to the analysis of an indefinite plurality of concrete cases, and which formulates in pure,

---

[6] Parsons, *ibid.*, p. 610.
[7] *Ibid.*, p. 604.

logically consistent form certain elements that are relevant to the understanding of the several concrete situations ... *these* are the general concepts necessarily involved in the logic of empirical proof ..."[8] Without in any sense detracting from Weber's formulation, it may be of interest to note that Dilthey also conceived of the "type" in ways similar to Weber. Dilthey held that it is of the very nature of human understanding (1) to see things against the background of a type, according to the way they fit into or deviate from it, and (2) thereby bring into sharp contrast that which is regulative and normative in a certain group of individual traits. Seeing things according to types, for Dilthey, not only fulfills a requirement of thought, but is the best way of setting forth uniformity, circumstances and destinies. Dilthey was thus not utterly an exponent of historical uniqueness as a consideration of his '*Verstehen*' doctrine alone might lead one to believe.[9]

An example of a general ideal-type Weber employs would be, say, the concept of economic rationality. This concept defines what would be perfectly rational economic behavior, that is, the concept defines a norm of rationality. Even though this norm might never be attainable in practice, Parsons notes, "it makes sense as a limiting case— in much the same way as the physical concept of a frictionless machine which would involve no transformation of mechanical energy into heat."[10] The general ideal-type, then, has possible empirical reference.

General ideal-types play a central role in scientific explanation. As in the example given, the ideal norm of rationality is of aid in "understanding the normative orientation of action. For this purpose it is convenient to take the case where the norm in question is conceived as perfectly realized; in this way, as Weber often notes, it is easiest to determine the role of other factors in terms of departure of the concrete case from the state of realization of the norm." At this point Parsons discusses Weber's schema of logical proof which, in all of its details, is of no concern here. Only one part of

[8] *Ibid.*, pp. 605–606.
[9] See Parsons' comments, *ibid.*, p. 634ff. See Dilthey, *Gesammelte Schriften* (Leipzig/Berlin, 1923), vol. v, p. 280ff.
[10] Parsons, *op. cit.*, p. 607.

Parsons' discussion of Weber is now pertinent, and that is the part which concerns Parsons' analysis of the 'general ideal-type.'[11]

The general ideal-type is, in the terminology of logic, a "class" concept or a "universal" of which the specific facts in question constitute a "particular" subsumed, so to speak, under it. Since it is a universal, the general ideal-type is applicable to an indefinite number of particular cases. But as this general ideal-type is formulated by Weber, it does *not* include in its formulation a set "of specific values of the elements relevant to the description of particulars in the class." If the general ideal-type were to include specific values of the elements, then it would be extremely limited and would probably not be a *general* type at all. "It contains no concrete facts. What it does contain is a *fixed set of relations* (possibly including variation within certain limits) of these values of elements . . . The *relations* between the values of the analytical elements which are important to the formulation of the type are always the same whatever may be their particular values and those of other elements."[12] Parsons' example of this is as follows: economic rationality, as mentioned before, is an example of a general property of action systems. "It is a property of the type of action Weber has described as traditionalism. Indeed this type involves . . . the maximization of economic rationality. But the maximization of economic rationality alone is not an adequate description of the type of action Weber had in mind. It is action which is economically rational relative to a traditionally fixed standard of living, that is, not relative to *any* given ends whatever but relative to a system of ends in which the property of traditional fixity is maximized. It is the *combination* of these two specific properties which defines the (traditional) type. But so long as this condition is given there is room for wide variation in the concrete instances in other respects, as in the concrete content of the ends and the particular features of the situations." The Silesian mowers, whom Weber analyzes in another context, are an example of this type. "The type is equally applicable to American miners whose consumption habits and whose situations, in so far as they are relevant to securing a fixed income, are widely different."

11 *Ibid.*, pp. 610–615.
12 *Ibid.*, pp. 615, 616–617.

E

Notice here that in the general ideal-type "the elements are related to each other in a particular combination. Traditionalism exists only in so far as, if economic rationality is maximized, the fixity of the standard of living is also maximized at the same time."[13]

General ideal-types, as in the example given, appear to be somewhat similar to "laws" in the physical sciences. That is, while they are not always identical to physical laws in logical form, they are meant to be identical in logical function. What is wrong with them? Parsons has said virtually throughout his entire intellectual career, in the early work being considered now and again almost thirty years later, that ideal-types, "though legitimate . . . have certain limitations and constitute only one of a number of the necessary theoretical components of the social sciences."[14] If one were to stop theoretical thinking with the formulation of ideal-types, or class universals, several unfortunate consequences would follow.

(1) Since the ideal-type embodies fixed relations between the values of its analytical elements, its employment alone, Parsons argues, "is one of the *principal sources of bias in empirical interpretation*." For example, Parsons believes that Alfred Marshall was most likely correct in his view that increasing rationality is an inherent tendency of human action. "But," Parsons observes, "he failed to see that this trend need not lead to free enterprise; it is not in the least incompatible, for instance, with an Indian caste system . . . (which) . . . may well differ from free enterprise in the scope of considerations brought within the range of economic calculation, but not necessarily in the degree to which the typical individual attains a norm of economic rationality within the scope of its application to him at all."[15]

(2) Although types are indispensable to scientific analysis, it is not possible to stop analysis merely with types. Each type concept is a unit of analysis by itself, but "the values of the general elements concerned are not always combined in the particular way that any one type concept involves; they are independently variable over a wider range." Therefore, if scientific analysis were to be restricted

13 *Ibid.*, pp. 616–617.
14 Parsons, essay in *Daedalus*, cited in ch. II, *supra.*, p. 60.
15 Parsons, *The Structure of Social Action*, pp. 619–620 (my emphasis).

only to "types," it would be necessary to have a different and separate type "for every possible combination of relations between the values of the relevant elements . . ." And if a different type would have to be formulated for every different combination of values of relevant elements, the result would be an unbridled "type atomism." Then, if the types are used exclusively (that is, if they are "reified"), the consequence is either a "mosaic theory of history or a rigid evolutionary scheme."[16] But there are yet further consequences:

(3) If theoretical work *stopped* with the formulation of ideal-types, Parsons argues, the types could then never be systematically classified. This would make history merely a process of "shuffling ideal-types, as *units*."[17] But what would it do to society? The same *logical* consequences holds for the analysis of society if scientific theories of society were limited to those of the "middle-range." If such theories could not be systematically classified and related to each other, it would follow that society would be merely an aggregate of 'shuffling' middle-range theories, as units. Parsons' "debate" —if it may so be called—with Merton on this issue occurred some ten years after the publication of his first major work. But since the point of his dissatisfaction with theories of the "middle-range" is identical with the point of his dissatisfaction with theories formulated exclusively as ideal-types, his comments are apposite here. Parsons states: "It is my contention that the time has passed when individual theories must be so particularistic that they must lack the common foundations which are necessary to make them building blocks in the same general conceptual structure, so that *theoretically* the development of our science may, to a degree hitherto unknown, become cumulative."[18] We may take it that Parsons' contention would apply not only to theories composed of ideal-types, or theories of the "middle-range," but to theories whose "class universals"

---

[16] *Ibid.*, pp. 618–621.

[17] *Ibid.*, p. 626.

[18] See Parsons' 1947 essay, "The Position of Sociological Theory," reprinted in *Essays in Sociological Theory Pure and Applied* (Glencoe: The Free Press, 1949, 1st edition), p. 14, also p. 4. Parsons made similar comments in his 1950 essay, "The Prospects of Sociological Theory," reprinted in the second edition of his *Essays*, 1954, p. 352.

consist of a specific "Geist" as well. However, there are dangers far more ominous than a mere type, Geist, or middle-range theory atomism that will follow from a failure systematically to classify the types and thus relate them to each other.

(4) The dangers, as Parsons sees them, may be made more apparent by recapitulating Weber's conception of value-relevance. Briefly and again: Weber held that a social scientist's values unquestionably direct his interest to certain problems. His observations, however, are then directed by the problem he has formulated. If his observations are verified, then the conceptual scheme in which terms he has formulated the problem is vindicated and the scheme may be judged to have yielded valid knowledge. Problems, however, and the conceptual schemes in which they are formulated, vary directly with differences in interest between social scientists. Since not all social scientists are interested in the same things, there is a relativity of problems and therefore also of conceptual schemes. This means that the "same" concrete materials "will give rise not to one historical individual but as many as there are points of view from which to study it."[19] General concepts of some sort will be developed in the process of analyzing an historical individual and comparing it with others. It does not follow, however, that in the numerous processes of analysis that occur only one uniform system of general concepts will be developed; there will of course be as many general concepts as there are points of view significant to knowledge. But, Parsons argues, "however different from each other the conceptual schemes are, in terms of which knowledge has been formulated, they must if valid be "translatable" into terms of each other or a wider scheme. This implication," he urges, "is necessary to avoid a *completely* relativistic consequence that would overthrow the whole position."[20] Parsons makes this point several times throughout his first work and it would seem to be of considerable—possibly of paramount—epistemological significance to him.[21] Although the method Parsons advocates to avoid a complete relativism may seem strange (the conceptual schemes "must if valid be "translatable"

---

[19] Parsons, *The Structure of Social Action*, p. 593.
[20] *Ibid.*, pp. 600–601 (my emphasis).
[21] *Ibid.*, pp. 600, 601, 638, 754–756.

into each other or a wider scheme") I shall attempt in the immediately following to set out uncritically what Parsons seems to mean by this.

Unfortunately, Parsons does not discuss the relativistic dangers in any great detail but refers to them as they are represented in Mannheim's and Durkheim's versions of the sociology of knowledge. The issue here, so far as I can make out, is this: if a relativism is introduced into scientific knowledge, it must not go so far as to impugn the claims of knowledge to validity. And validity involves at least two "components": for the moment let me call them "objectivity" and "universality." Weber's formulation is explicit and almost adequate, in Parsons' estimation, in providing a justification of knowledge to "objectivity." Weber held, that is, the logic of verification to be identical for any science, natural or social.[22] Since it is identical, the logic of verification provides a stable, non-relative reference point for all the sciences. But "objectivity" and "universality" are not the same things. We may know, for example, that a proposition is "objective" if we have evidence for it; but this does not mean we will therefore know the range of its application. Weber's version of the general concepts needed in social science does not go far enough, and we shall see in a moment why Parsons thinks this is so. As Weber formulated them, the concepts are too restricted in their "universality," for they are "class concepts." For example, there may be a general "ideal-type" of the sun by which we may characterize any number of suns, but no other objects. What is needed is a universal (or universals) the scope of which is unrestricted or infinite. A pure universal of the sort, say, as the term "mass" is not restricted to any one class of objects: the sun, any planet, or any physical object *has* a mass but is not a mass.[23] The pure universal, in logical terms, is a universal of predication. This universal refers to properties or qualities of objects rather than to a class of objects.

[22] *Cf.* Parsons' discussion, *ibid.*, pp. 581–600; *cf.* Weber, *op. cit.*

[23] Parsons, *ibid.*, p. 616. The materials for a large part of this discussion are drawn from ch. XVI of *The Structure of Social Action*. I have also drawn pertinent materials from Parsons' "Introduction" to *Max Weber: The Theory of Social and Economic Organization* (New York: Oxford University Press, 1947).

Parsons' formulation is here substantially identical to Hempel's and Oppenheim's, referred to earlier, who define a pure universal, or a universal of predication, as a "statement (which) does not require reference to any one particular object or spatio-temporal location"; for a universal of predication refers to qualities and is therefore not restricted in scope. Terms such as "warmer than," "longer than," "green," are examples of qualitative predicates. These are the sorts of terms employed in "fundamental" scientific laws, and it is through 'fundamental' laws that "derivative" laws containing class universals may be logically organized. Parsons' view of the logical functions of 'fundamental' laws is couched in a like manner.[24] But the critical question would then be whether all 'derivative' laws—embodied in specialized, restricted theories —can indeed be fully organized within a system of laws containing universals of predication. Apparently, the occurrence of such thorough organization is questionable even for the physical sciences. We do not have to rely solely upon the analyses of Thomas Kuhn's more recent and much contested work to raise this question. Ernest Nagel, whose work is rather less controversial than Kuhn's, has also noted: "it is today (1961) far from certain that such statements as Kepler's are in fact logically derivable from fundamental laws *alone* . . ."[25] How does this lack of derivation affect the knowledge proposed by more restricted theories?

If knowledge were to be restricted to conceptual schemes containing *only* ideal-types—that is, to schemes composed entirely of class universals—the schemes would be incomparable. In fact, the ideal-types developed by Weber have been manifestly defined in such terms that they are not comparable to each other. The ideal-type of traditionalism, for example, is a class universal composed of a fixed combination of elements. As defined previously, traditionalism is completely different from the combination of elements which make up the class universals, say, of the ideal-types of charisma or bureaucracy. "Thus": should more than one 'ideal-type' be used in

24 *Cf.* Hempel and Oppenheim, cited in ch. 2, *supra.*, pp. 341ff; see also Parsons, *The Structure of Social Action*, pp. 615–617.

25 *Cf.* Thomas Kuhn, *The Structure of Scientific Revolutions* (Chicago: Phoenix Books, 1964); see also Ernest Nagel, *The Structure of Science* (New York: Harcourt, Brace & World, Inc., 1961), pp. 57–59.

the analysis of the "same concrete materials"—as has happened, and as we have every reason to expect will continue to happen—very different and competing assertions will be made of the "same" materials. The assertions may then appear to contradict each other. But the dilemma is that each of the assertions, if verified, will have evidence in its favor. They are all "objective." There may be as many 'ideal-types' of the sun, for example, as there are points of view from which to see the sun. Unless each of the conceptual schemes from which the assertions are made can be grounded in some way, that is, interrelated and compared with each other, we will have no sure way of assessing the scope of any of the assertions. From each conceptual scheme it may be said: "the sun is x," or "the sun is y," or "the sun is z." And each assertion may be as "true" (that is, as 'objective' and 'verified') as one could wish. We need only recall in this connection Alfred Marshall's contention that increasing rationality will lead finally to free-enterprise. Given Marshall's assumptions—namely, *his* "ideal-type" of free enterprise—this would appear as the only correct conclusion. Yet, as Parsons analyzes the matter, Marshall's conclusion is clearly one-sided. The consequence may then well be (and historically has often been) an endless logomachy of conflicting claims and counter claims from which we would have some justification in coming to a skeptical conclusion as to the general validity of any of the claims that has been made. We would then have some warrant to saying each of the assertions is peculiarly arbitrary, for each assertion is "valid" only in terms of the conceptual scheme from which it has been generated, and each scheme in turn is "relative" only to those values which have directed its formulation. Change the values and we will get a change of schemes and a change of assertions.

This argument is hardly novel in the social sciences. Gouldner, for example, has argued similarly in an earlier essay. In agreement with Arthur O. Lovejoy, Gouldner suggests that "every theory is associated with, or generates, a set of sentiments which those sub-scribing to the theory could only sense." He then suggests that the 'unwarranted conclusions' are not merely a result of logical errors but of biases connected to that set of sentiments which constrain other considerations. His commentary is directed to some of the work of Max Weber, Talcott Parsons, Roberto Michels and Philip Selznick.[26] These conclusions constitute precisely the outcome of the radical relativism embodied in Mannheim's conception of the sociology of knowledge. Parsons is completely explicit in wanting to avoid this outcome.[27]

However, Mannheim was well aware of this outcome and made a statement that is suggestive of a possible way by which it may be avoided. I do not for an instant believe that Parsons is attempting to carry out Mannheim's program; there is no evidence that can be found to this effect. But the program Mannheim briefly formulated, and did not develop, virtually matches the statement quoted above by Parsons as to the method required to avoid a complete relativism (conceptual schemes "must if valid be 'translatable' into each other or a wider scheme"). It is worth noting Mannheim's program here for it is descriptive of what Parsons is trying to do. In Mannheim's formulation:[28]

... when observers have different perspectives, "objectivity" is attainable only in a roundabout fashion. In such a case, what has been correctly but differently perceived by the two perspectives must be understood in the light of the differences in structure of these varied modes of perception. An effort must be made to find a formula for translating the results of one into those of the other and to discover a common denominator for these varying perspectivistic insights.

There is some small irony in the fact that Merton once expressed agreement—never since disavowed—to the conception of validity presently under discussion. In an early essay of Merton's, published in 1941, he briefly criticizes Mannheim's epistemological views, takes issue with one of Mannheim's conceptions of validity, and states: "One may grant different perspectives, different purposes of inquiry, different conceptual schemes and only add that the various results be translatable or integrated before they are judged valid.[29]

[26] Gouldner, "Metaphysical Pathos and the Theory of Bureaucracy," *American Political Science Review*, vol. 49, 1955, pp. 496–507.

[27] Parsons, *op. cit.*, p. 601, esp. note 2; see also p. 480.

[28] Mannheim, *Ideology and Utopia*, cited in ch. 2, *supra.*, p. 270.

[29] See Merton, "Karl Mannheim and the Sociology of Knowledge," in *Social Theory and Social Structure* (Glencoe: The Free Press, 1957), p. 504, note 21.

On this point there are no differences between Mannheim's, Parsons' and Merton's conception of validity. Are we then to await the finding of a 'common denominator' before we assess the validity of theories of the middle-range?

Whether this conception of validity can be upheld, notice, however, that Parsons is responding to the relativistic consequences of historically formed social thought. Mannheim once likened this consequence to a "thorn in the flesh."[30] To dub Parsons' work "unhistorical"—without further ado—is, I believe, to do an injustice to his acute awareness of the apparent dilemmas of the 'historicity' of social thought. I have endeavored in this and the preceding chapter to bring out the range of Parsons' awareness of difficulties historical influences may place upon thought. All parts of his work, I would contend, may be interpreted as an effort to come to terms with these influences. Parsons' work cannot be well understood unless there is a recognition that he constantly grapples with the problem of the relativity of social and historical knowledge.

The fact that Weber did systematically relate the numerous 'ideal-types' he had formulated to each other, Parsons asserts, means that he must implicitly have held to a more general scheme. There are grounds for believing that Weber was opposed to a conceptual scheme that was "too general" for fear the scheme would be so abstract it would never be able to get to the historical individuals he was interested in comprehending. His general ideal-types, therefore, were intended to provide a conceptual "half-way" point, so to speak, between the historical individuals of his interest and such logical universals (of predication) as are found in the basic laws of some of the physical sciences. But Weber could not have related the general ideal-types to each other, Parsons insists, without using a system of classification containing concepts of greater generality than any of the ideal-types themselves.[31]

Parsons sees as one of his tasks the making of that more general

[30] See Mannheim's letter to Kurt Wolff, reprinted in part in "The Sociology of Knowledge and Sociological Theory," *Symposium on Sociological Theory*, edited by Llewellyn Gross (Evanston: Row Peterson and Company, 1959), p. 571.

[31] Parsons, *op. cit.*, pp. 633–634; *cf.* his "Introduction" to *Max Weber: The Theory of Social and Economic Organization, op. cit.*, pp. 27–28.

scheme explicit—not, of course, for the sake of scholarship alone, but for the purpose of achieving valid knowledge. Parsons believes this achievement requires two things, and they may be stated again: the provision of a means for the intellectual control of all our verified observations of social action—that is, the construction of a comprehensively general theory of society from which all verified observations may be deduced; and the justification of that theory against skeptical, relativistic attacks. Parsons' early means-end schema is intended to clear the way for the fulfillment of both requirements. Weber's argument that the logic of verification is applicable to all the sciences is convincing and provides one of the non-relative reference points needed, so Parsons agrees, "to bring order into the mass of relative propositions that constitute scientific knowledge." But another non-relative point may be provided, Parsons believes, by "the main formal outline of the means-end schema (for this schema) is inseparable from the conception of action. Relativity," Parsons insists, "can only apply to the specific modes of its application . . . not to the formal scheme itself so long as the conceptual scheme of action is employed at all."[32]

The next chapter will set out the ingredients of this other non-relative point and present further grounds by which Parsons' work may be appraised. We shall see that Parsons attempts not only to develop a concept of "the social," but also seeks to establish a supreme intersubjectivity of all views of the social, and thus to find a condition of rapport between all the 'verified' singular views of the objects of society that have so often been pitted against each other throughout history.

[32] *The Structure of Social Action*, p. 638.

CHAPTER FOUR

The First Solution
of the Epistemological Problems

Parsons is after a framework of basic categories which must be necessarily presupposed in any theory of social action. He offers us in his first work the means-end schema as precisely that framework. The schema consists of the categories of means, ends, conditions and norms. Of course there have been and still are theories of "action" which openly repudiate one or more of these 'basic' categories. And those theories are to be heard expounded by adherents of idealistic, utilitarian and positivistic traditions. But a determinate explanation of social action, for which purpose those very theories have been formulated, cannot be had unless the facts to which each of the categories refers, with no exception, are explicitly taken into account. This is Parsons' thesis throughout. And yet further, Parsons shows that Marshall, Pareto, Durkheim and Weber, starting from very different positions, were each moving in their work towards a recognition of the theoretical importance of all the categories. Parsons defines the categories as follows: Every action is performed by someone who acts, an actor. His action involves, first, an *end*, or future state of affairs, towards which the process of action is directed. Second, action always occurs under some *conditions* which the actor cannot alter. Such conditions constrain his actions. Third, action always involves *means* employed for the achievement of an end. Fourth, action, however, always involves *norms* which direct the selection of some means over others that are available. "Action," Parsons tells us, "must always be thought of as involving a state of tension between two different orders of elements, the normative and the conditional. As process, action is, in fact, the process of alteration of the conditional elements in the direction of conformity with norms."[1]

This framework of categories, then, is a "step" in the direction of that "common denominator," referred to in the previous chapter, which will allow particular theories of social action to be translated into each other. I shall quote again Parsons' claim cited near the beginning of this study: "There are no group properties that are not reducible to properties of *systems* of action and there is no analytical theory of groups which is not translatable into terms of the theory of action."[2] Parsons, however, is explicit in cautioning against the confusion of this framework with a causal explanation. A causal explanation will come later when a system of variables, corresponding to the categories of the framework, will be constructed. The framework prepares the way for such a construction, but by itself explains nothing. What is it then? The framework is a necessary "preliminary to explanation," Parsons maintains, for "facts cannot be described except within such a schema . . . their description within it has, in the first instance, the function of defining a 'phenomenon' which is to be explained."[3]

Social action, then, is defined in terms of the framework Parsons has given us. That framework delineates the anatomy or structure of an action. And even though any action is a "whole," it is made up of parts which the categories define. A causal explanation, on the other hand, will require that the framework of 'basic' categories be reworked into a framework of analytical elements. This means that every concrete entity described in terms of this framework must have general properties. "It is these general (properties) of concrete phenomenon relevant within the framework of a given descriptive frame of reference, and certain combinations of them, to which the term "analytical elements" (is) applied . . . An analytical element . . . is an abstraction because it refers to a general property while what we actually observe is only its particular 'value' in the particular

---

[1] This quotation may be found in *The Structure of Social Action, op. cit.*, p. 733. The material preceding is an extremely brief summary of pp. 44, 45, 49, 697–726.

[2] *Ibid.*, p. 747, italics in the original.

[3] *Ibid.*, pp .28–30.

case."[4] Analytical elements, as Parsons conceives them, are those universals of predication which were discussed in the preceding chapter. As an analytical framework the action schema "takes on a different meaning from that which it has as a descriptive schema. Its elements have causal significance in the sense that variations in the value of any one has consequences for the values of the others."[5] The specific consequences will of course be determinable by "laws" (rules) which relate the elements to each other. However, Parsons is emphatic that in his first work he has not constructed a "system of variables" or analytical elements and therefore we may take it he has so far not produced any of the logical predicates of his interest. His statements concerning such a system are essentially programmatic; its development is to be carried out by following the "analytical program" as it was called in an earlier chapter.

Is the action framework, then, merely a set of definitions? Does the framework do no more than indicate the mode of "general relations of the facts implicit in the descriptive terms employed"?[6] Consider these further claims Parsons makes of the framework: "It is *impossible*," he says, "to have a meaningful description of an act without specifying all four (ends, means, conditions, norms) . . . These underlying features of the action schema," Parsons maintains, ". . . do not constitute 'data' of any empirical problem; they are not 'components' of any concrete system of action." What do they then constitute? The underlying features of the action schema (ends, means, etc.), Parsons says, "are in this respect *analagous* to the space-time framework of physics. Every physical phenomenon *must* involve processes in time, which happen to particles which can be located in space. It is *impossible* to talk about physical processes in any other terms, at least so long as the conceptual scheme of the classical physics is employed. Similarly, it is *impossible* even to talk about action in terms that do not involve a means-end relationship . . . It is the *indispensable* logical framework in which we describe and think about the phenomena of action." Finally, Parsons says, "the fact that whenever the general action schema is used at

---

[4] *Ibid.*, pp. 34–35.
[5] *Ibid.*, pp. 750ff.
[6] *Ibid.*, pp. 28–30.

all phenomena are described in terms of this common frame of reference means that whatever level of analysis is employed there is a common structure of all systems of action."[7]

I have quoted Parsons at length, and underscored certain of his formulations, for a purpose. For Parsons appears to be making claims that bear a close resemblance to the claims made by Kant of his a priori categories, namely, that they were the "indispensable principles" underlying all knowledge. The language Parsons uses is of course reminiscent of the Kantian language. But far more than this, Parsons sees *his* action scheme to be *analagous* to the space-time framework of physics which is "necessary" for the comprehension of every physical phenomenon—precisely as Kant claimed it to be. It is this framework which (in the classical physics) makes it *possible* to "talk about physical processes." And it is Parsons' framework which (in action sociology) makes it possible to talk about social processes.

There is more here, however, than a mere "formal identity" of claims between Kant and Parsons. The claims are made in the face of extraordinarily similar *epistemological* problems. Let us consider for a moment Kant's approach to these problems for this will illuminate, I believe, Parsons' own efforts. For Kant, the problems centered presumably on the unbearable skepticism issuing from Hume's analysis of knowledge.[8] Hume, it will be remembered, attempted to show that by our sense impressions alone we perceive no more than a succession of events, or an association of events, but no necessary connection between them. And if there is indeed no necessary connection between events, Hume argued, then we cannot justifiably speak of their causes. There are no *theoretical* grounds, so Hume held, by which we can prove that a mere sequence or associ-

---

[7] *Ibid.*, pp. 732ff (my emphasis).

[8] . . . "presumably," because there remains some question as to just how much of Hume's work Kant knew, although Kant does say it was his remembrance of Hume's analysis that awoke him from his dogmatic slumbers. See Kant, *Prolegomena to Any Future Metaphysics* (New York: The Liberal Arts Press, 1951), p. 8. *Cf.* Norman Kemp Smith, *A Commentary on Kant's Critique of Pure Reason* (New York: The Humanities Press, 2nd edition, 1950), p. xxv et seq., who presents some evidence that Kant was familiar with Hume's *Enquiry* before he undertook his first great *Critique*.

ation of events will ever be repeated. The sun may have arisen every day in the past, with no known exceptions, but this fact does not logically compel us to deduce that it will rise tomorrow. No evidence can be found in this fact for such a conclusion. Of course we may expect that the event will occur, and, in fact, to act at all we must believe that it will occur. But our expectation is based, perhaps, on habit or faith. It cannot be rationally defended. At best we may give our expectation a pragmatic excuse, but that excuse is certainly not logically convincing. Scientific laws, therefore, and for Hume this meant the Newtonian physics especially (although he admired Newton's work), are not theoretically justified in their claim to universal validity. From this a theoretical skepticism descends upon scientific knowledge, for since we cannot justifiably assent to anything beyond the impressions of our senses, the order which scientific knowledge imposes upon our sense impressions cannot be rationally upheld.[9]

The epistemological import of Hume's doctrine—skepticism—is identical to the skepticism that follows from the historical views discussed earlier. Kant answered Hume by arguing that, in the first instance, we never receive merely "raw" sense impressions. We always order or organize our impressions. We have an experience of objects; that is, we have knowledge of them, and not mere sensations. But how is experience of objects—knowledge—possible? For Kant, it was the mind itself that contributed forms necessary for such an ordering of impressions. Kant asked: What are the conditions of sense experience? His answer, which need not be examined in detail, is that there are categories of cognition, or of the understanding, which are fundamental to any sense experience. Without such categories we could have no experience. Experience is always formed, and it is the categories of the understanding (space, time, etc.) that make formed experience possible. And experience formed by these categories gives us "nature," for nature, as Kant conceives it, consists of *phenomena* under laws *given by the understanding*. The categories are not derived from any experience, but are the

[9] David Hume, "An Enquiry Concerning Human Understanding," reprinted in *Hume: Theory of Knowledge*, edited by D. C. Yalden-Thomson (Austin: University of Texas Press, 1953).

necessary principles applicable to all experience. This is the meaning of that famous epigram with which Leibniz retorted to Locke and which is sometimes aptly used to render the general import of Kant's epistemology: "There is nothing in the intellect that has not been before in the senses, except the intellect itself and the forms of the intellect."[10] We could not think or know without such forms. Knowledge necessarily rests upon the principle of causation and derives its unity from it. But the categories, conditions or principles of knowledge are not applicable to the *objects* of our experience. And nature is not to be confused with those objects. We can never find the categories in the objects themselves. The categories only apply to, and they are constitutive of, human knowledge. The specific contents of our sense experience may vary without limit, but the categories which make it possible for us to have a sense experience are permanently fixed—that is, they are universal to any human experience. The a priori categories, then, are distinguished by their universality and necessity, for they refer not to the objects of experience but to the form all our experience takes.[11] Thus it is impossible to think of any physical process in terms that do not involve the categories of space, time, causality, etc.; these are the categories that are presupposed, a priori, universal and necessary bases for our experience of any physical process whatsoever.

This, in exceedingly brief compass, is Kant's argument. From it the skepticism advanced by Hume concerning the way we order our knowledge may be vanquished. That way is not arbitrary, as Kant believed he had shown; the order of our knowledge is not based on faith, habit or pragmatic exigency, nor is it based on any connection presumed to be inherent in the objects of knowledge. Kant fully agreed with Hume that such objects can never be shown to be connected in themselves. A view of knowledge which wishes to limit knowledge only to its objects—that is to say,

[10] "Nihil est in intellectu, quod non fuerit in sensu," Locke cited with approval. "Excipe: nisi ipse intellectus," Liebniz added. Liebniz, *New Essays Concerning Human Understanding*, translated by Alfred G. Langley (New York: Macmillan Co., 1916, 2nd edition), II, 1 paragraph 2.

[11] *Cf.* Kant's *Prolegomena, op. cit.*; also his *Critique of Pure Reason*, translated by Norman Kemp Smith (New York: St Martin's Press, 1956), esp. pp. 592ff, 621ff, 653ff.

an exclusively empirical view—is bound to issue in a far-reaching skepticism. The order and unity of our knowledge are brought into existence by the contribution of the mind—the a priori, universal and unchanging forms by which we synthesize our impressions and which alone make knowledge possible.

One of the differences between Kant and Parsons is that Kant is known to have been a "critical idealist," whereas Parsons claims his own metaphysical position to be that of "analytical realism."[12] There is a certain overlap in meaning between "analysis" and "critique," but the metaphysical differences between idealism and realism are quite beside the point for this study. What is important, and what this study claims, is that Parsons is essentially adopting Kant's *logical* strategy (not metaphysical, not substantive) in order to overcome the skepticism entailed in those relativistic doctrines that have been reviewed. In the logic of their procedure, that is, in the way they attempt to base their claims, Kant and Parsons are remarkably similar. Each is concerned with establishing categories necessary for knowledge. Furthermore, each claims, very generally speaking, that without a certain set of categories—the action schema for Parsons in his first work, the space-time framework for Kant— knowledge, either of social action or physical processes, will not be possible.

To prevent possible misunderstanding, another note of qualification may be helpful. The claim of Parsons that is so similar to Kant's should be distinguished from two other assertions Parsons makes of his means-end schema. As was seen in the previous chapter, Parsons also argues that cumulation of knowledge will not occur unless a more general scheme is employed by which 'data' may be compared. Furthermore, Parsons also argues that unless there is a basis for cumulation of knowledge, the validity of the small bits of knowledge garnered will be brought into question. These arguments should be considered separate from Parsons' assertion that it is impossible even to describe or think of the phenomena of action without pre- supposing his means-end framework. *This* is the assertion that so closely parallels Kant's. The other two are not to be found in any of Kant's works so far as I know.

[12] Parsons, *op. cit.*, pp. 753ff.

F

The close similarity of the claims made by Parsons and Kant is more than a matter of mere terminological coincidence. In part, the similarity is an outcome of the fact that each attempts to solve the "same" general problem, namely, epistemological skepticism. The nature of the problem for Parsons has been set forth in some detail, although not nearly so extensively as is to be found in his own work. The nature of the problem for Kant has been very briefly sketched but sufficiently, it is hoped, so that it may be seen how very similar the problem is, in general terms, to the problem faced by Parsons. However, the similarity of the claims made by Parsons and Kant is also in part an outcome of the fact that each attacks the problem in much the same way. It is true that nowhere in his work may Parsons be found to say outright that he follows Kant's procedure. However, he does say in his first work that his procedure is not altogether without precedent. His procedure is 'formally identical' to Simmel's attempt to gain a basis for sociology as a special science. Although Simmel's *conclusion* is not acceptable to him, Parsons asserts that "it was founded on sound insight," and Parsons believes that his own view "may be regarded as a restatement of (the) sound elements (of Simmel's thought) in more acceptable terms. The main difficulty for Simmel," Parsons notes, "was that the view he took of the other social sciences precluded relating his concept of sociology to other analytical social sciences on the same methodological level. To him sociology was the only abstract analytical science in the social field."[13]

Parsons' identification of his procedure with Simmel's, in his first work, is fortunate for a number of reasons. First, Simmel explicitly bases his procedure on Kant's, that is, Simmel pursues an avowedly a priori course. And if the law of transitivity holds, it must follow that Parsons also bases his procedure on Kant's. This *perhaps* clinches the argument that Parsons' manner of theorizing, at least in the early work, is cast in the a priori mode. But I would consider the argument "clinched" only when: (1) the a priori mode is made clear, and (2) Parsons' own mode of theorizing has been shown to correspond perfectly to it. Second, the particular work by Simmel to which Parsons refers is much simpler in detail than virtually any of

[13] *Ibid.*, pp. 772ff.

Parsons' work (and it is certainly much simpler than any of Kant's). Exhibiting the logic of this procedure, then, will be greatly facilitated by examining Simmel's application of it. And this is the remaining task of the present chapter. Once the characteristics of this procedure are fixed, I shall turn to an examination of Parsons' later works with the aim of seeing the extent to which they conform to this procedure. Then, finally, the procedure itself will be assessed and its virtues or shortcomings may be transferred directly to Parsons' work, so far as applicable, to enable us to come to some evaluation of it.

An elucidation of the a priori mode should help further to clarify the sense in which Parsons embarks upon the construction of a scientific theory. So far, I have restricted my commentary largely to epistemological issues. However, we should recall that Parsons sees his means-end schema in at least a double aspect. The schema provides epistemological services by being an "indispensible logical framework." But it will also provide scientific services when the schema is properly reworked into a system of analytical elements, for then the elements should be able to supply causal explanations. Let us now examine Simmel's view.

The A Priori Mode in Simmel's Work.—Parsons refers to the first chapter of Simmel's *Soziologie* in which a precedent for his own procedure may be found. That chapter is entitled "How is Society Possible?"[14] and the title alone is suggestive of a Kantian influence. But Simmel's answer to the question is different in substance from the answer Kant gave to the similar question he asked of knowledge. The a priori which Simmel constructs does not refer to the unchanging and universal forms of the mind that order and unite our

---

[14] This chapter is omitted in the English translation of Simmel's work by Kurt Wolff, entitled *The Sociology of Georg Simmel* (Glencoe: The Free Press, 1950). However, it appeared much earlier in English translated by Albion Small under the same title as given above in *The American Journal of Sociology*, 16, 1910–1911, pp. 372–391. All references are to Small's translation, although I have emended the translation somewhat. Two commentaries on Simmel have been occasionally helpful. *George Simmel 1858–1918*, edited by Kurt Wolff (Columbus, Ohio: The Ohio State University Press, 1959; and *Georg Simmel*, edited by Lewis Coser (New Jersey: Prentice Hall, Inc., 1965). The essays by Alfred Mamelet, "Sociological Relativism," and F. H. Tenbruck, "Formal Sociology," in Coser's volume are instructive.

sense impressions. "On the contrary," Simmel says, the unity of society "is realized by its elements without further mediation (by the mind), and with no need of an observer, because these elements are consciously and synthetically active. The Kantian theorem, 'Connection can never inhere in the things, since it is only brought into existence by the mind,' is not true of the societary connection which is rather immediately realized in the 'things'—namely, in this case the individual souls."[15]

Although Simmel's answer is different in substance from Kant's, Simmel follows the same general logical procedure that Kant employed. Simmel asserts: "The sociological apriorities will have *the same double significance* as those 'which make nature possible''; on the one hand they will more or less completely determine the actual processes of socialization, as functions or energies of the psychical occurrence, on the other hand they are the *ideal logical presuppositions* of the perfect—although in this perfection never realized—society."[16]

Simmel defines society as a consciousness of unity on the part of its members. His concern is to find the a priori conditions effective for this kind of consciousness. Briefly, Simmel believes they are as follows: (1) perceptually and cognitively we always reconstruct individuals into 'types'—officers, merchants, Protestants, Catholics, Jews, Republicans, Democrats, officials, teachers, students, and so on. This means, according to Simmel, that "the individual is rated as in some particulars different from his actual self by the gloss imposed upon him when he is classified in a type..." But the individual is always more than any characterization we may give of him. For every characterization of an individual is simultaneously abstract and general. As the characterization is abstract, we miss a part of the individual; as the characterization is general, it extends beyond him. But "...those changes and reshapings which prevent this ideal (that is, complete) representation (of the individual), are precisely the conditions through which the *relationships* we know as the strictly social become possible—somewhat as with Kant the categories of reason, which form the immediately given into quite

[15] Simmel, *ibid.*, pp. 373–374.
[16] *Ibid.*, p. 377 (my emphasis).

new objects, alone make the given world a knowable one."[17] (2) No individual engages himself fully in social life. Every member of a group, says Simmel, "is not only a societary part, but beyond that something else." And this is the second social a priori: "That the individual, with respect to certain sides of his personality, is not an element of the group, constitutes the positive condition for the fact that he is such a group member in other aspects of his being." That is to say, what the individual is as a socialized being "is determined or partially determined (by what he is as a) non-socialized being."[18] The distinction Simmel makes here is somewhat similar to the distinction made by George Herbert Mead between the "I" and the "me." Mamelet's commentary may be useful at this point: "This concept (of Simmel's) is clearly the theoretical complement of the first (given above). It limits itself to postulating the existence of . . . something in and of itself and thus provides a notion which the first category could not contain . . . The extra-social self maintains a reciprocity of interaction with the social self (the extrasocial self constituting the result of social influences; the social self devoting itself to directing the reaction of the individual to those influences.)"[19] (3) Since society is a structure of unlike elements, then the final a priori which provides the individual with a foundation for belonging to society is expressed as follows: "That each individual, by virtue of his own quality, is automatically referred to a determined position within his social *milieu*, that this position ideally belonging to him is also actually present in the social whole—this is the presupposition from which as a basis the individual leads his societary life." But Simmel quickly observes and emphasizes the fact that if social reality were fully to be conditioned by this principle, there would then be a perfect *society*.[20] And by "perfect" Simmel means something like "complete" or "fully realized."

From the foregoing it should be apparent that the a priori mode does not involve the fallacy of begging the question, or of *petitio principii* as this fallacy is formally identified in logic texts. The

---

[17] Simmel, *ibid.*, p. 381 (my emphasis).
[18] Simmel, *ibid.*, pp. 381–382.
[19] Mamelet, *op. cit.*, p. 72.
[20] Simmel, *op. cit.*, pp. 387–389.

strategy of the a priori does not consist of simply assuming that which is to be proved. Simmel does not prove there is a consciousness of unity because there is a consciousness of unity—which is of course no proof at all. For epistemological purposes, the three a prioris sketched above may be taken to provide the logical presuppositions which organize our *knowledge* of society. But for scientific purposes, these very same a prioris, when properly converted, express the necessary conditions for the occurrence of the event, namely, society defined as consciousness of unity. The logical form in which the scientific proposition may be put is: If items (1), (2) and (3), above, are *not* present in some degree, then a society in some degree will *not* be present.

But for scientific purposes, notice, the necessary conditions must be vindicated in some other way than by the claim that they are logical presuppositions. That is, if the a prioris are indeed necessary conditions *for the event* we must be able to show that when those necessary conditions are absent, the event will not occur; or, what is saying the same thing, that when the *event* occurs, the necessary conditions will be present. And to be able to show that would certainly be showing a great deal. If certain conditions are necessary for any society, they are then supra-historical and they must underlie any and every society in history. A great deal of Simmel's work was undertaken in order to examine the plethora of social forms which exist but which nevertheless have their anchor in just these necessary conditions.[21]

However, there is a difference between providing a necessity of thought and providing a causal explanation of events, and there is a danger this difference will be obscured when there is an interest in trying to do both. Simmel was outspokenly opposed to epistemo-logical relativism and his apriorities were intentionally constructed to overcome such relativism.[22] But Simmel also clearly asserted that the sociological apriorities "will more or less *completely determine* the actual processes of socialization ..." What does "completely

---

[21] *Cf. The Sociology of George Simmel, op. cit.*, in conjunction with Simmel's essay, "How is Society Possible," *op. cit.*

[22] Simmel, *The Sociology of Georg Simmel*, pp. 1–6; *cf.* Mandelbaum's account of this opposition, cited in ch. 2, *supra*, pp. 101–119.

determine" mean here? This expression cannot mean that the apriorities are *only* 'necessary conditions' for the event, although the categories in which the apriorities are expressed may very well be necessary for *thinking* of the event. If the apriorities were only necessary *for* the event, however, then, when they were actually present as conditions, it would not follow that the event had to occur. But if the sociological apriorities are indeed completely determining of the event (not less and not more), they must be both necessary *and* sufficient conditions of the event.

The distinction between the two types of conditions is occasionally confused. However, they are presented in elementary logic texts under discussions of material implication in the following way. A *necessary* condition is expressed, "if not n, then not q." When the necessary condition, "n," is absent, then the event, "q," *cannot* occur. But when the necessary condition, "n," is present, then the event for which it is necessary, "q," may *or may not* occur. A *sufficient* condition for an event, on the other hand, is stated as follows: "if s, then q." When the sufficient condition, "s," is present, then the event, "q," *will* occur. But when the sufficient condition, "s," is *absent*, then the event, "q," may or may not occur. An incisive illustration of the distinction between necessary and sufficient conditions is given by Cohen and Nagel:[23]

... the existence of sexual desires is sometimes said to be the cause of the family as a human institution on the ground that in the absence of sexual desires there could be no marriage. Evidently, however, all that is thus shown is that the existence of sexual desires is a *sine qua non* or *necessary* condition for this institution. But in order to explain adequately the family in terms of sex, it must be shown that man's sexual nature is by itself a *sufficient* condition for the existence of that institution, and this is not true if we can find sex expression without family life.

There is some ambiguity in Simmel's account of the apriorities as

[23] Morris Cohen and Ernest Nagel, *An Introduction to Logic and Scientific Method* (New York: Harcourt, Brace & Co., 1934), p. 388; *cf.* Irving M. Copi, *Symbolic Logic* (New York: The Macmillan Co., 1954), pp. 18ff; Alice Ambrose and Morris Lazerowitz, *Fundamentals of Symbolic Logic* (New York: Rinehart & Co., 1948), pp. 82ff.

conditions of the event he wishes to explain. In his version, they "more or less" determine consciousness of unity. There is no question, however, that as they are a priori, they must be *at least* necessary conditions. If they did not fulfill this requisite, any number of other conditions would be possible, and the way would again be opened to an unbridled relativism. The apriorities must be necessary conditions, that is, because in the statement form of a necessary condition, "if not n, then not q," the following implication, "if q, then n," is of course valid. Following Cohen and Nagel, if sexual expression is a *necessary* condition for family life, then, whenever we find family life we will expect to find sexual expression. Thus, whenever we find a consciousness of unity, we will expect to find the apriorities Simmel has brought forth (if they are indeed necessary conditions).

I do not mean to belabor elementary logical distinctions. My only intention is to clarify the differences between necessary and sufficient reasoning—differences which, although elementary, are important but nevertheless confused at times—and to lay the ground for evaluation of the a priori mode. An event or a phenomenon cannot be explained adequately by reference only to its necessary conditions. To repeat then: when in fact a necessary condition for an event has been construed, to the extent that it is necessary, that condition is implied (or is present) whenever the event occurs. But the inverse, as the illustration from Cohen and Nagel[24] should make clear, does not hold. For this reason a necessary condition of society may be said to underlie every society in history, for any society must entail that necessary condition. Thus, given any society, the apriorities Simmel has formulated are involved if they are indeed necessary conditions. And it is in this sense that all social forms have their anchor in those necessary conditions. But whether the apriorities are also sufficient conditions is, to put it most leniently, an open question, at least in Simmel's formulation of them. And until we are able to decide that they are also sufficient conditions, we cannot justifiably assent to the claim that when they are present a society will also be present. In fact, Simmel is clear in later portions of his

---

[24] *Cf.* Cohen and Nagel, Copi, Ambrose and Lazerowitz, *op. cits.*

Soziologie that the apriorities are not sufficient conditions, for by themselves they cannot explain variations—the manifold 'forms'— among societies.[25] From this we may conclude that the logical form in which the apriorities are cast (as conditions) is not now in conformity to the minimal form a causal explanation should take.

Summary Comparison of Parsons and Simmel.[26]—The categories Simmel has constructed have two references. They have a "logical" reference in that they are at least some of the presuppositions necessary to unify our knowledge of society. They have an empirical reference, at the same time, in that they express some of the "energies" in or of the objects necessary to interrelate such objects to one another. As Simmel phrases it, "the functions or energies of the psychical occurrence" more or less make for a consciousness of unity. Such unity among people (the "objects") is what we term society. This unity is brought into existence by those very objects and without further mediation by any observer's mind. Parsons makes a similar distinction in his discussion of a theoretical and empirical system, cited earlier in this study. A theoretical system is a body of logically interrelated propositions. This is not a "real" system for it states no facts; it merely defines general properties of empirical phenomena and states general relations between their values. An empirical system, on the other hand, *is* a body of interrelated phenomena. But the relatedness or unity of such phenomena is not a derivative of the mind; our theoretical formulations do not unify social phenomena for they are unified of themselves. Parsons very briefly postulates "an external world of so-called empirical reality which is not the creation of the individual human mind and is not reducible to terms of an ideal order"[27]—rather unlike Kant here. In this respect Parsons differs metaphysically from Kant. Sim-

[25] See Simmel's essay, "On the Significance of Numbers for Social Life," in *The Sociology of Georg Simmel, op. cit.*, pp. 87–104. Some commentators have questioned the alleged universality and necessity of the *a priori* categories. *Cf.* Mandelbaum, *op. cit.*; also Hans Freyer, *Soziologie als Wirklichkeitswissenschaft* (Leipzig/Berlin: B. G. Tübner, 1930), pp. 46ff.

[26] *Cf.* Donald N. Levine, *Simmel and Parsons: Two Approaches to the Study of Society* (University of Chicago: Unpublished Doctoral Dissertation, 1957) for more explicit sociological comparisons.

[27] Parsons, *The Structure of Social Action*, p. 735.

mel's difference from Kant is perhaps somewhat less than Parsons, for he drew the same distinctions as Parsons but limited their application only to social phenomena. (Simmel is considered to have been a "neo-Kantian.") Despite these differences in emphasis between Parsons and Simmel they are nevertheless rather close, epistemologically, and it may be stated once again that for Parsons as for Simmel, the categories underlying a theoretical system are a priori, and they are in fact held to be necessary to organize our knowledge.

However, we must not forget that Parsons has urged in his first work that his "logical framework" of action not be confused with a causal explanation of social action. A causal explanation, he has said, will come later with the construction of a system of analytical elements corresponding to the categories of the "logical framework" he has developed. The categories of the logical framework are held to 'make it possible' to talk of social action, but they do not constitute a "theoretical system." Notice, therefore, that here Parsons has *reversed entirely Kant's epistemological procedure.* For Kant undertook his analysis only *after* the Newtonian physics had been constructed and was available for his inspection. The a priori categories Kant brought to light were the categories applicable to the Newtonian physics and thus depended for their elucidation upon the prior occurrence of that physics! But the convergence Parsons claims to have found in the works of Marshall, Weber, Pareto and Durkheim—whether or not he is correct in his findings—cannot be taken to provide in advance the epistemological foundations of Parsons' future scientific work. For such foundation also depends for its elucidation upon the actual occurrence of that work. I would remind the reader of a statement Parsons makes in the very same work that proffers us the categories without which it is 'impossible' to speak of social action. "It must never be forgotten," Parsons said, "that there may well be hereditary elements which 'drive' behavior in conformity . . . with a rational norm . . . (and) . . . insofar as this is true, whatever subjective aspect there is to action will turn out, on thorough investigation, to be reducible to terms of nonsubjective systems. The test is always whether an adequate explanation of the concrete behavior in question can be attained without reference to the elements formulated in concepts with an inherent subjective reference."[28] Although I have little sympathy with positivist thought, I must conclude that the certainty with which Parsons asserts the sweeping epistemological claims of his "logical framework" is not warranted—and, in fact, that the claims cannot yet be supported.

Before turning to an examination of Parsons' later theoretical work, a brief "metaphysical interlude" is in order so that various metaphysical criticisms of Parsons may be examined and dispensed with.

[28] *Ibid.*, p. 701.

CHAPTER FIVE

Metaphysical Interlude

Parsons has never, to my knowledge, set down a full scale metaphysical program. Doubtless he has metaphysical views, and they play some role in his sociological thinking. However, the exact definition of this role is obscure, perhaps for the reason that neither Parsons, nor the few commentators who have glanced at this aspect of his thought, have been sufficiently interested to pursue the metaphysical questions beyond a few cursory observations. Although I shall not deviate from this approach to the subject, I should like to point out insufficiencies even within the compass of the meager study the subject has received so far, and chart a few preliminaries which may be suggestive of a more intensive investigation that could be undertaken.

Let us begin with Parsons' view of the interrelations of empirical and theoretical systems. "The systems of scientific theory," Parsons says, "are obviously not this external reality itself, nor are they a direct and literal representation of it ... They stand, rather, in a functional relation to (external reality), such that for certain scientific purposes they are adequate representations of it." Scientific theories are therefore not merely fictions as, in fact, Weber held. The applicability of scientific theory to 'external reality,' please note, "implies that empirical reality is in this sense a factual order." Furthermore, continues Parsons, the order of empirical reality "must be of a character which is, in some sense, congruent with the order of human logic. Events in (the empirical world) cannot occur simply at random, in the sense which is the negation of logical order." But this formulation, Parsons hastens to add, should not be taken to imply the proposition that "reality is exhausted by its *congruence* with the kind of ideal systems accessible to the mind in its scientific

phase ..."[1] Parsons' main emphasis here is upon the regulated composition of the empirical world, and of our knowledge of that world
—and to understand the principles of the composition of the social
world is the supreme concern of all his intellectual efforts. I believe
that by paying attention to Parsons' conception of the range of
application of such non-fictional principles we may gain access to his
metaphysical views.

Gouldner has referred to Parsons' definition of an empirical
system in one of his earlier essays. He asserts that if Parsons does
indeed define such a system "realistically"—as above—this definition
would (1) unwittingly retain "vestiges of eighteenth century usage,
referring to a 'natural' system which is somehow there 'in itself' in
a realistic sense ..." and (2) "be radically at variance with Parsons'
methodological position, which is predominantly constructionist."[2]
There is no doubt that Parsons is 'realistic' in all of his work in the
sense given by his comments cited in the text, and "analytical" as
well in the sense developed in chapter II, above. Unfortunately,
Gouldner does not discuss what is "wrong" with a "realistic" view
of an empirical system, or how this view is radically at variance
with a constructionist or analytical approach. Parsons' conceptions
are abstractions, but they are abstractions, presumably, of something
which is there in society to be abstracted. Where is the dilemma?
In any case, Parsons' view is very close to Whitehead's on these
matters, and he has explicitly acknowledged his debt to Whitehead's
conception of an organic system very early in his own work. By
noting this affinity I do not mean to defend Parsons' view, only to
express puzzlement at Gouldner's perhaps too cryptic commentary,
for Whitehead was of the twentieth century and Parsons has openly
and steadfastly modified his "realism" with the methodological
adjective, "analytical."[3] Lest my own remarks appear too cryptic
and my puzzlement puzzling, I refer the reader to Ernst Cassirer's
history of philosophical thought in the eighteenth century, *The
Philosophy of The Enlightenment*. In this work Cassirer reveals

---

[1] *The Structure of Social Action, op. cit.*, pp. 753–754 (my emphasis).
[2] "Reciprocity and Autonomy in Functional Theory," *op. cit.*, p. 252.
[3] *Cf.* Whitehead, Alfred North, *The Concept of Nature* (Cambridge: Cambridge University Press, 1920), ch. I; *cf.* Parsons, *op. cit.*, pp. 32ff.

with unparalled clarity how the method of analysis advocated by Newton did not merely permeate eighteenth-century thought on the most varied subjects, including sociological and political inquiries, but indeed the analytical method was believed to be the most fitting complement of the "realistic" view. The fusion of 'positivism' and 'rationalism' as pertains to sociological thinking is to be found in Condillac's *Treatise on Systems*, among other works of that period. Certain portions of Condillac's *Treatise*, in fact, bear a distinct resemblance to Parsons' later version of a social system—extraordinary as this may appear at a first sighting which does not also see the impact of the Newtonian method upon Condillac's and Parsons' thinking. It is this impact which accounts for the similarity between them, I believe, rather than any literal influence of Condillac's thinking upon Parsons. Condillac's fomulation of society is replete with such system concepts as equilibrium, interdependence, reciprocity, etc. These are "mental constructions" without doubt, but they are held to elucidate the empirical relations that exist in the body of society. The intellectual aim of Condillac, and also of Montesquieu in the *Spirit of The Laws*, is not limited simply to an empirical description of the forms and types of society and state constitution, but includes an attempt, as Cassirer puts it, "to construct them from the forces of which they are composed."[4] The constructionist methodology in these instances has thus certainly not been believed to be 'radically at variance' with a realistic conception of an empirical system.

Gouldner's commentary nonetheless touches desultorily on metaphysical issues which have received somewhat more sustained attention in other hands. In a study completed in the early 1950's, Roscoe J. Hinkle, Jr. takes notice that in his first work Parsons has been influenced by Kantian and neo-Kantian thought.[5] Whether Parsons' theory of knowledge is Kantian in all respects has not been a matter of interest to the investigation being conducted here. But Hinkle apparently believes Parsons' thought is thoroughly "Kantian." The issue is complex and, short of a different investigation from the one this study (or Hinkle's) undertakes, it is very

---

[4] *Op. cit.*, p. 20; see also p. 17, 21, 22.
[5] *Theories of Social Stratification in Recent American Sociology* (Madison: The University of Wisconsin, unpublished doctoral dissertation, 1952).

difficult to come to a clear decision on the matter. What does
'Kantian' refer to? Even if Parsons' epistemology is Kantian, does
it follow irrevocably that his metaphysics is also Kantian? As we will
remember, Kant does not hold his theory of the knowledge of the
phenomenal world to be fully sufficient for the knowledge of human
beings. For Kant, man participates simultaneously in two worlds,
that of nature and of freedom. Kant believes an additional concept,
other than the concept of nature, is therefore required to render
man's activities intelligibly. In his third great critique, *The Critique
of Judgment*,[6] Kant provides us with the concept of purposive*ness*.
Notice the stress: this is *not* purpose. However, the concept of
purposiveness is not deemed to be constitutive of man as the a priori
categories are constitutive of the phenomena of nature and therefore
also of man as he too is a phenomenon of nature. The concept of
purposiveness is a *heuristic* concept; it aids us in investigating man's
activities as they move in the direction of a moral order. Kant sees
man in a state of tension between that which is, nature, and that
which ought to be, morality. However, the concept of the will—not
purposiveness, but the will—is, for Kant, beyond all theory. The
will acts but it cannot be known. Kant is therefore a "radical
voluntarist." Hinkle observes that Parsons formulates his action
framework in somewhat similar terms—that the categories of
Parsons' voluntaristic and slightly later functional theory invoke
different principles for the explanation of different orders of phenomena: natural scientific principles for the explanation of the conditions of action, "subjectivistic" principles for the explanation of
the goals and normative constraints upon action. To speak loosely,
voluntarism and functionalism are both "teleological." Given this
duality of principles, Hinkle concludes, the major metaphysical
underpinnings of voluntarism and functionalism, in Parsons' versions of them, may then be traced back to the tenets of German
idealistic philosophy.[7] I do not believe this conclusion is warranted
for several reasons which pertain to the meanings of "dualism" and
"idealism" respectively:

---

[6] Translated by J. H. Bernard and published in New York by the Hafner
Publishing Co., 1951.

[7] Hinkle, *ibid.*, pp. 227–237.

(1) An economist may very well argue that the physical principles, the laws, determining the path of a particle are not applicable to the determination of the market price of any product. The latter is presumably a function of the laws of supply and demand which are not physical laws in any substantive sense. Does this make the economist a "dualist"?

(2) Kant holds the concept of purposiveness to be merely heuristic; it is not constitutive of man's activities. This concept is, so to speak, a fiction—necessary, perhaps, for the comprehending of man's actions, but a fiction nevertheless. Parsons, on the other hand, is outspokenly opposed to fictional concepts—he is an "analytical realist." To the extent that a theory is confirmed that theory is congruent with some aspects of reality. The propositions of a theory, when verified, then represent constitutive aspects of external or empirical reality. If the distinction between constitutive and heuristic concepts is consistent with Kant's metaphysical dualism, what are we to make of the fact that Parsons opposes such a conceptual distinction for the deciphering of his metaphysics?

(3) As many of the foregoing citations show, Parsons considers none of the major metaphysical positions sufficient, for each one leads—when taken singly—to untenable constraints upon the explanations of social phenomena. Since Parsons manifestly attempts to *interrelate* such phenomena conceptually, for he believes—please notice—that they are interrelated in reality, evidence may be found in his work of some affinity with all of the metaphysical views which have been the ground, as it were, for all of the phenomena of his interest. Parsons does not totally reject positivism, nor does he totally reject idealism. They both refer to something real; they are both, therefore, important. Unfortunately, each involves an explanation of the "real" in a manner which would exclude the real as well as the explanation of the other. And Parsons wants to include them both. Does this make Parsons a "dualist" and an "idealist"? Hinkle concludes in the affirmative, but he does not explore these matters at length. The question of Parsons' "dualism" (but not idealism) is answered affirmatively and at greater length in a more recent study.

In an essay published in 1963 John Finley Scott asserts that in his early work Parsons is at least an explicit metaphysical dualist because he believes "the world of space and time and the world of ultimate value are equally and irreducibly real . . ."[8] Scott emphasizes that in his early work—most of which has been under consideration in the previous chapters of this study—Parsons is a metaphysical dualist for the reason that he sees each of the worlds as independent of the other. And Scott is certainly right, for Parsons does see each of the "worlds," as real worlds, to be independent of one another. But Parsons sees them as much more, and I believe Scott's claim that Parsons' metaphysics is dualistic to be too simple a formulation. We need but recall: first, that the action schema for Parsons, when developed and converted into a system of analytical elements, will have explanatory power in the sense that variations in the value of *any one* element have consequences for the values of the others. The elements refer to the different, but equally real, worlds. Second, Parsons is explicit that in an empirical system, by which he means a real system, the elements are not merely independent but *interdependent* as well.[9] Gouldner, who champions the view of variations in the interdependence of system elements, has in numerous of his writings argued that Parsons always casts the relations of system elements to be—in Gouldner's words—"mutually interdependent." And thus, according to Gouldner, Parsons' formulation would ignore the independence and the autonomy of system parts.[10] But this argument, I believe, is at least equally simplistic, for it neglects precisely that part of Parsons' characterization which Scott has seen correctly. It would be best to quote Parsons directly:[11]

It is one of the commonest but most serious of fallacies to think that *inter*dependence implies absence of *in*dependence. No two entities *can* be interdependent which are not at the same time independent in certain respects. That is, in general terms, all independent variables are, by virtue of the fact that they are variables in a system, interdependent with other variables. Independence in the sense of complete lack of inter-

---

[8] "The Changing Foundations of the Parsonian Action Schema," *American Sociological Review*, vol. 28, #5, October, 1963, p. 724.

[9] Parsons, *op. cit.*, pp. 25, 750ff.

[10] Gouldner, *ibid.*, pp. 254ff; *Cf. The Coming Crisis of Western Sociology, op. cit.*, ch. 6, section entitled "system interdependence."

[11] Parsons, *op. cit.*, p. 25.

G

dependence would reduce the relations of two variables to sheer chance, incapable of formulation in terms of any logically determinate functions. A dependent variable is, on the other hand, one which stands in a *fixed* relation to another such that, if the value of *x* (an independent variable) is known, that of *y* (the dependent variable) can be deduced from it with the aid of the formula stating their relation, and without the aid of any other empirical data. In a system of interdependent variables, on the other hand, the value of any one variable is not completely determined unless those of all the others are known.

In Parsons' view, set out near the beginning of his first major study, an empirical or real system is not sufficiently characterized by referring *solely* to the independence of its elements.

We may infer from the formulation just quoted that a dependent variable is to be found expressed, among other places, in the relations constructed by way of "ideal-types"—if we also keep in mind Parsons' analysis of such constructions which I have briefly re-capitulated in the third chapter, above. For ideal-types, remember, embody fixed relations between their elements. Parsons' notion of interdependence can be grasped more fully, I believe, if we refer to the reservations he has advanced as to analyses limited to ideal-types. An interdependent variable would be one term in a far more complex construction in which the number, value and relation of terms to each other may be constantly reformulated. Any single formulation of such a complex construction may be likened to an "equation" incapable of being solved if the values of two or more terms remain unspecified. An "equation" of this sort would express the relations and values ('weights') of so-called 'real' societal parts at a specific moment in time. In principle, therefore, the values as well as the relations of the terms of the equation need not remain constant, but may change with every reformulation of the equation. This principle, clearly implied in the above quotation, would help assure that the 'equation' remain 'congruent' with every societal change. Parsons' conception would thus admit that at different historical times certain societal parts *may* have a greater impact than others in affecting the character of the society in question. Far from denying 'determinate-ness' in the social world, this conception attempts to point to the complexity and variability of the interdependencies, the 'real' determinations, that are believed to exist in the social world. The goal of analysis is to unravel these complexities for our understanding—however distant this goal may be.

Is Parsons' notion of interdependence finally transfixed by pinning it bluntly to a so-called "metaphysical vision of the oneness of the world"?[12] Gouldner's animadversion suggests either that Parsons believes the social world is everywhere made of the same stuff, or that the social world is everywhere put together in the same way. And if Parsons indeed holds to either of these elemental views of the 'metaphysical domain,' it would not be surprising if his view of interdependence were then correspondingly elemental—consisting, as Gouldner says, of the notion that system elements are 'mutually interdependent,' thus obscuring recognition of the autonomy of system parts. From the foregoing, however, it would seem to be closer to the mark to say that Parsons has a vision of the variegated stuff of the world held together in numerous ways. Difficult though it may be to strike a phrase which will encapsulate the intricacies of this vision with some semblance of accuracy, I would suggest that Parsons envisions the several syntheses of things in the social world rather than the mere sameness or unchanging unity of such things. This formulation is not intended to prevent anyone's metaphysical hackles from rising. Certain of the historicists, as we may remember, would perhaps raise severe objections to any holistic view, whether of a single system or multiple systems. And certain contemporary positivists would bristle even at the whisper of a metaphysical notion of whatever kind. But here we would embark upon lines of thought that would lead us away from the matters presently under discussion.

Parsons' view of interdependence, then, also does not lend support to Scott's contention that his metaphysics is dualistic. We should recall Parsons' emphatic statement, cited in the second chapter, above, that it is necessary to go beyond metaphysical dualisms. For, once granted, these dualisms result in the 'eclectic' view that the relations between the 'spheres' are non-existent, or are no more than accidents—haphazard, random touchings that elude any theoretical grasp. In the face of this seeming conceptual embarrassment, and perhaps also because he has a metaphysical presentiment of their

---

[12] Gouldner, *The Coming Crisis* . . . , *ibid*.

relations to begin with, Parsons has said that he would endeavor to give an account of "the specific modes of interrelationship between the two" spheres. But that the spheres may be interrelated does not mean that one can be reduced to another. Parsons has been equally emphatic that each sphere has its own distinctive, irreducible principle of organization, as Scott has correctly noted. In opposition to the reductionist thesis, however, Parsons has also said that the 'real' system he will attempt to construct will be seen to "have properties that are emergent only on a certain level of complexity in the relations of (parts) to each other." An example Parsons gives of an *emergent* property is as follows. If one describes a "single rational act with a clearly defined immediate end and a specific situation with given conditions and means," it would not be possible to decide "whether or in what degree (that single act) is economically rational." For, Parsons maintains, "the economic category involves by definition the relation of scarce means to a plurality of different ends. Economic rationality is thus an emergent property of action which can be observed only when a plurality of unit acts is treated together as constituting an integrated system of action. To carry unit analysis to the point of conceptual isolation of the unit act is to break up the system and destroy this emergent property."[13]

Notice that in this early conception Parsons is hardly so nominalistic as Martindale once characterized the philosophical import of this phase of his work.[14] But notice also that the epistemological status of "emergence" in Parsons' usage is not altogether clear. Perhaps an emergent property cannot be readily foretold. Does this mean an emergent property cannot be causally explained? Ernest Nagel, for instance, believes "the claim that there are emergent properties in the sense of emergent evolution is entirely compatible with the belief in the universality of the causal principle, at any rate in the form that there are determinate conditions for the occurrence of all events."[15] In Parsons' sketchy formulation, an analysis of the determinants of so-called emergent properties would not seem to be precluded—at least in principle. For although "emergence" in

[13] Parsons, *ibid.*, pp. 739ff.
[14] *Cf.* note 19, ch. I, *supra*.
[15] *The Structure of Science, op. cit.*, p. 377.

Parsons' usage may be related to an evolutionary conception, it is most doubtful that conception has anything in common with the philosophical doctrine of creative evolution as espoused, say, by Bergson. Nothing Parsons says resembles the idea of a "vital impulse" propelling the emergence of new properties. The analysis of a given emergent property, in Parsons' example, would refer us solely to a specific type of social organization with which that property is associated. We shall encounter the emergence notion again, later, when we examine Parsons' views of social evolution. At that point, the sense in which emergent properties are "explained" will have become clearer. For the moment, I would suggest that Parsons' recent attention to the question of social evolution had received some ground work thirty years earlier, and does not represent a startling departure from his theoretical concerns.

One may object to the account Parsons has given of the relations he believes to exist between the dualistic spheres. One may claim, with some justice, that his account remains largely programmatic. But if one wants first to discern Parsons' metaphysical premises, however complex they may be, the statement of his intention as well as his repeated citations are enough to provide some clue to his metaphysical affinities. Kindred premises have been more fully elaborated by a philosophical source close to hand.

There is a charming story told of Alfred North Whitehead. In one of his seminars at Harvard, almost fifty years ago, Whitehead was discussing the idea of an organic system. To underline a point, so the story goes, he smote his forehead with the palm of his hand, peered at his students, and owlishly intoned: 'By this action I have affected the farthest star in the universe.'[16] In the multiplicity of the "real worlds" Parsons alludes to, in the fact of their syntheses and interdependence—their *ordered* relations to each other—that he stresses, in the analytically abstract approach he advocates and the "correspondence" theory of truth he assumes, the outline of Parsons' metaphysics, though barely preceptible, shows a marked resemblance to the views of Whitehead. This can be seen merely by a further perusal of Whitehead's work that Parsons cites so frequently and

[16] As told by Professor Marvin Farber to one of his seminars, almost fifteen years ago.

positively, *Science and The Modern World*.[17] Whether Parsons
follows Whitehead completely cannot be judged short of very
careful comparisons which it is not the purpose of this study to
undertake. But to the extent that he does follow him—and in the
superficial respects considered here, it would seem a considerable
extent—I do not believe it is appropriate to cast Parsons' metaphysics
in the terms of the more common philosophical nomenclature.
Whitehead's views, for example, have been described under various
headings: 'panpsychic realism,' 'neo-idealism,' etc—as can be seen
from an examination of learned commentary upon his work.[18] Since
Parsons is far less explicit than Whitehead with respect to his metaphysical premises, greater caution should be exercised in attempting
to characterize them, or their changes over the years if there have
indeed been any.

The philosophy of organicism, I would venture, has most likely
been the chief metaphysical influence upon Parsons' sociological
thought. But although of undoubted pertinence in arriving at a full
understanding of Parsons' (and perhaps anyone's) thinking, the
metaphysical questions shall be pursued no further here. For whatever Parsons' metaphysical affinities may be, and however they may
have affected his epistemological and scientific thinking, Parsons
shall not be assessed in this study as a metaphysician. My sole aim
shall be to assess how well, and in what manner, he achieves his
most explicitly stated objectives: the provision of an adequate explanation of social action. Let us now turn to an examination of his
scientific thought.

[17] *Op. cit.*, especially chs. 1xff.
[18] *Cf.* certain of the essays in *The Philosophy of Alfred North Whitehead*,
edited by Paul Arthur Schilpp (New York: Tudor Publishing Co., 1951),
especially by F. C. S. Northrup, "Whitehead's Philosophy of Science," and
C. I. Lewis, "The Categories of Natural Knowledge."

CHAPTER SIX

The Functional 'Solution' of the Scientific and Epistemological Problems

I have contended that the logical manner of all Parsons' formulations, epistemological and sociological, has remained constant, and that this constancy may be interpreted as the outcome of his attempt to solve the alleged epistemological dilemmas of historical relativism and positivist and idealist reductionism. In the fourth chapter a sketch of the "a priori mode" of reasoning, as it was there called, was developed, and the distinction drawn between a necessity of thought and an adequate explanation of events. If the categories involved in non-reduced propositions of society can be shown to be necessities of thought, and certain of these propositions shown to be universal in scope, many of the 'imperialist' claims made by historicists and positivists will then lose their force, and some of the so-called epistemological dilemmas ensuing from these claims will have been resolved. My contention that Parsons' substantive work, his thinking on social action itself, is everywhere cast in the "a priori mode" must now be given support. The objective of this and the following chapter will be to examine the gamut of Parsons' sociological formulations to gauge the extent to which he relies upon "necessary reasoning." Wherever possible, Parsons' later comments shall be inspected to see whether he continues to endeavor to subdue the dilemmas he believes to be involved in the historicist and positivist standpoints. One question vital to an internal critique of Parsons' work, discussed in the second chapter, namely, whether Parsons succeeds in his aim of providing an adequate causal explanation of the facts of his interest, shall be postponed for later discussion. But I would remind the reader that a large part of Parsons' case against historicism and positivism rests on his argument that neither standpoint alone has conceptual resources adequate for an explanation of the full range of the facts of social action. Therefore, until Parsons does come forth with an adequate causal explanation of such facts, his own work will be open to much the same charge he has levelled against the historicist and positivist views. And being open to this charge, the 'eclecticism' that he seeks to overcome between the standpoints by interrelating them in the form of adequate causal statements will thus also remain unvanquished on his own grounds. For none of the standpoints can be shown to be necessary for the sorts of causal statements Parsons wishes to construct until those statements have actually been constructed. But eclecticism, however discomfiting, at least consists in a truce by which is kept alive thought systems whose value may well be destroyed in 'imperialist' ventures. Those who deem each of the incompatible thought systems valuable but limited, who would not deny or tamper with any of the realities to which all of the standpoints refer, may find in Parsons' work the virtue of an argument that the mere thinking of the full range of the facts of social action requires the resources of all the standpoints, whatever the form of the statements such thinking may take, and however unrelated these statements may be. An impoverished world, they may say, is too high a price to pay for mere consistency.

Parsons does not hold fast to the means-end schema outlined in his first work. In his next major works he shifts away from the details of that schema and once again sets out to construct a comprehensive theory of systems of social action. He believes this shift "constitutes a new and extended statement of the subject matter of *The Structure of Social Action*."[1] At the same time, however, the shift is not indicative of a radical departure from the basic concerns entertained in his 1937 work. In 1950, for example, Parsons again notes that "social scientists are plagued by the problem of objectivity in the face of tendencies to value bias to a much greater degree than is true of natural scientists. In addition, we have the problem of selection among an enormous number of possible variables. For both these reasons," he urges, "it may be argued that perhaps theory is even more important in our field than in the natural sciences." A few pages later, in the same essay from which I have just quoted, he

[1] Parsons, *The Social System* (Glencoe: The Free Press, 1951), p. ix.

states: "The basic reason why general theory is so important is that the cumulative development of knowledge in a scientific field is a function of the degree of *generality of implications* by which it is possible to relate findings, interpretations, and hypotheses on different levels and in different specific empirical fields to each other. If there is to be a high degree of such generality there *must* on some level be a common conceptual scheme which makes the work of different investigators in a specific sub-field and those in different sub-fields commensurable."[2] Again, Parsons stresses the importance of a common theoretical perspective, for in his collaborative work with Shils the following is asserted: ". . . it might be fairly claimed that the present scheme offers the basis of an important advance toward the construction of a unified theory of social science . . . It should thus contribute substantially to the development of common way of looking at the phenomena of human conduct."[3]

All of the preceding statements have substantially the same import as the ones Parsons made more than a decade earlier in his critique of Max Weber's 'ideal-types,' reviewed in chapter III. Parsons' concern continues to be at least partly epistemological, for "general theory," he says at the outset in his joint work with Shils, "will facilitate the control of biases of observation and interpretation which are at present fostered by the departmentalization of education and research in the social sciences."[4] General theory, we may safely infer, will aid us in ascertaining the scope in which more particularistic theories are definitely valid. That 'common way of looking at the phenomena of human conduct' continues to be precisely the measure invoked to translate limited but 'valid' theories into each other's terms, and thus overcome a threatening skepticism which dogs them all so long as they remain relativistic, that is, not 'commensurable 'or 'untranslated.' Neither Parsons' desire to combat epistemological relativism, nor his conception of the condition for a victorious outcome, has wavered in the slightest from 1937 to 1951.

[2] Parsons, "The Prospects of Sociological Theory," in *Essays in Sociological Theory* (Glencoe: The Free Press, 1954), pp. 348, 352.

[3] Talcott Parsons, Edward A. Shils and others, *Toward a General Theory of Action* (Cambridge: Harvard University Press, 1952), p. 238.

[4] *Ibid.*, p. 3.

Parsons has of course changed in his substantive views during this period and in fact beyond it. His reasons for such changes shall be cited at appropriate points, for if they are not 'defensible' we may wonder whether a stable, general theory of the sort Parsons desires is possible. Even if his reasons are defensible, the question of the possibility of a *stable*, general theory remains open sheerly by virtue of the changes that have occurred in his own work. There is no doubt that he wants such a theory; that much is clear from the materials quoted so far. But there is some question whether such a theory is desirable or possible for the reasons and in the terms Parsons has advanced. These questions shall be deferred so that we may get on with an examination of the form of Parsons' sociological thinking. His principal works following *The Structure of Social Action* shall be examined for this purpose.[5]

Parsons is clear that although he does not cling to the means-end scheme, he has no intention of forsaking that scheme entirely. When used to analyze certain empirical problems, he says, "a certain awkwardness seems to have been involved in" the means-end scheme. But "gradually it became evident that the same conceptual scheme could be restated in a somewhat different form and perspective, with the result of bringing it much closer to current levels of empirical

---

[5] For convenience, the following works will hereafter be cited by the assigned letter:

(A) *Essays in Sociological Theory: Pure and Applied* (Glencoe: The Free Press, 1949).

(B) *Toward a General Theory of Action, op. cit.*

(C) *The Social System, op. cit.*

(D) *Essays in Sociological Theory* (1954), *op. cit.*

(E) *Working Papers in the Theory of Action*, with Robert Bales and Edward A. Shils (Glencoe: The Free Press, 1955).

(F) *Family, Socialization and Interaction Process*, with Robert Bales and others (Glencoe: The Free Press, 1955).

(G) *Economy and Society*, with Neil J. Smelser (Glencoe: The Free Press, 1956).

(H) *Theories of Society*, edited by Talcott Parsons, Edward A. Shils, Kaspar D. Naegele and Jess R. Pitts (Glencoe: The Free Press, 1961).

(I) "Evolutionary Universals in Society," *American Sociological Review*, vol. 29, #3, June, 1964, pp. 339–357.

(J) *Societies: Evolutionary and Comparative Perspectives* (Englewood Cliffs, New Jersey: Prentice Hall, 1966).

research and conceptual schemes..."[6] This different form and perspective is of course the explicit functionalism—or 'structural-functionalism'—associated with the bulk of Parsons' efforts. Let us now see what the problems are other than those already mentioned in this chapter which this somewhat new perspective is intended to solve, and the manner by which such a solution takes place.

The Problems and The Solutions.—The remaining problems are not new at all. They have all been encountered before. One of them is the 'problem of social order.' This problem concerns the patterns of real or empirical systems. Another way of stating the problem is to ask what are the conditions for the interdependence of the parts of a social system. "Interdependence," says Parsons, "consists in the existence of determinate relationships among the parts or variables as contrasted with randomness or variability ... interdependence is *order* in the relationship among the components which enter into a system."[7] Notice that the phraseology of this formulation of 1951 echoes the version of interdependence espoused by Parsons in 1937, mentioned in chapter V, from which we may infer a certain methodological continuity. But Parsons introduces an apparently "new" term which has at times ruffled certain of his commentators. For the conditions of order in the relations among parts which enter into a system, Parsons now says, also determine that system's *equilibrium*. Thus, Parsons is concerned with bringing to light the conditions of the very existence of such systems, for "in any system," he states, "... the conditions of equilibrium ... are in the last analysis the conditions of the system's being a system."[8] As can be seen, and as shall be seen more fully, Parsons employs the two terms, equilibrium, and interdependence, as equivalent expressions. Perhaps this new term to be used in sociological analysis is simply another resonance of the Newtonian influence upon Parsons discussed earlier. In any case, the minor tempest his usage of 'equilibrium' has occasioned in some quarters seems to me to arise partly from a lexical confusion, and is thus a consequence of reading into that term something Parsons does not mean. Parsons does not mean by equilibrium an

---

[6] A, p. viii.
[7] B, p. 107.
[8] B, pp. 107, 120.

utter lack of process. In fact, 'equilibrium,' in the sense of ordered
relations, can figure in an analysis of change, as Professor Robert
Nisbet has pointed out.[9] To the extent the squabble is merely
terminological, it lacks substantive interest. I shall return to the
notion of equilibrium later in this chapter.

Another problem, not stressed yet familiar, is to identify whatever
it is that is ordered. We will recall that one of the purposes of the
action framework was to identify the phenomenon to be explained.
Before we can speak of the conditions for the existence of a social or
any other kind of system, the system itself must be clearly defined.
Parsons now defines a system as the interaction of two or more units
in a state of bounded equilibrium. This means: (1) that there is no
change of state in the units of the system relative to each other, and
(2) that the "state of the system is limited in extension and the state
description of the system may be discriminated from that which is
non-system, namely, the environment."[10] This doesn't say very much.
At best, an intention is being expressed here, for we have yet to
discover whatever is ordered in the general way Parsons has conceived, and the principles upon which this order rests. Remember
that Parsons wants to develop at least a set of master terms to serve
as the basis for the construction of a 'unified theory' of social science.
His views of what constitutes equilibrium and boundary maintenance, of what is a system and what is a unit, should therefore pertain
to all of the domains of interest to the social sciences without
exception. Before exploring his new frame of reference which
articulates the subject matter of his concerns, and his explanation of
the occurrence of equilibrium, etc., it would be useful to distinguish
Parsons' treatment of a system from that of its units. For here too
there have been certain, perhaps understandable, confusions.

A *unit* of a system is simply that which is "treated as an elementary particle." A *system*, on the other hand, is defined as "two or
more units, $x_1, x_2, \ldots x_n$, related such that a change of state of any x_i
will be followed by a change of state in the remaining $x_j, \ldots x_n$

[9] *Social Change and History, op. cit.*, pp. 271ff, pp. 282ff.

[10] This characterization, and some of the following, is taken from Morris
Zelditch, Jr., whose compact summary of Parsons' and Bales's work on
equilibrium is reproduced as the second Appendix in F, pp. 401–408, with—
it must obviously be inferred—Parsons' approval.

which in turn is followed by a change of state in x_i, etc." This means, as Parsons illustrates it, that the "interaction of a small group of persons may be taken as a system, and their interactions classified with reference to the system they compose . . . (But) if one wishes to account for the properties of something formerly treated as a unit, in terms other than its membership in a system, then one *changes the point of reference*, and now treats the former unit as a system."[11] Every unit of a system is conceived to be a system itself to which the properties of interdependence and boundary-maintenance accrue by definition. Therefore, the relationship of units to each other is in fact construed to be a relationship of systems to each other. As every unit is a system, and as all systems are 'bounded,' every unit is perforce conceived to possess some degree of 'independence,' for any unit is distinguished from all other units and the 'environment'—again, by definition. There is some danger that upon entering this conceptual labyrinth one may never be heard from again unless drastic steps at simplification are taken. But any simplification, such as the various reductions discussed in earlier chapters, or some equivalent to these, such as an over-arching 'single factor' theory, would obviously destroy the entire conception. Apparently, even Parsons himself is not always impervious to taking measures of this sort, for a unit of a large-scale social system need not be reduced to such fixed designations as the 'role,' or the 'status-role,' as he occasionally has said.[12] A 'unit,' in principle, could as well refer to any social group, social class, organization, etc., so long as that 'unit' is interacting at least with one other unit to form an equilibrated system.

What is needed is some sure guide which will lead us from unit to unit, and one state of a system to another—that is, an identification of units and their interrelations. Parsons, in fact, points to a great variety of units and systems when he envisions the equilibrium of a large-scale society. Equilibrium in the case of this huge system is ". . . made up of many sub-equilibriums within and cutting across one another, with numerous personality systems more or less in internal equilibrium, making up different equilibrated systems such as kinship groups, social strata, churches, sects, economic enterprises

---

[11] F, pp. 401–402; E, p. 175; *cf.* the entire discussion in E, pp. 172–179.
[12] C, pp. 24–25.

and governmental bodies. All enter into a huge moving equilibrium in which instabilities in one subsystem in the personality or social sphere are communicated simultaneously to both levels, either disequilibrating the larger system, or part of it, until either a reëquilibrium takes place or the total equilibrium changes its form."[13] The actual concentration of an investigator upon a specific 'unit' or 'system' for study is likely to depend upon his interests, and also reflects the specialization of his training. Doubtless, value-relevance plays a role in directing interests as well. But all such units and systems, however they have been selected for study, must have an empirical reference, for Parsons conceives them to have properties of a certain kind. It must be borne in mind that included in Parsons' aim is the development of some set of universals of predication, qualities, applicable to all social objects (or 'systems'), the scope of which will not be restricted to any one class of such objects. Part of his case consists in identifying the range of pertinent units, systems and predicates; indeed, he provides a "catalogue" of qualities and classes of social objects to which I shall turn shortly in examining his 'frame of reference.'

Parsons' distinction between 'unit' and 'system,' and their interrelations, is explicitly formulated in organicist terms. The formulation is of course not new, nor does Parsons claim that it is. Much the same sort of formulation may be found in the literature of anthropology, biology and gestalt psychology, among other disciplines, and this idea has often been discussed by philosophers of science.[14] Although Parsons has held to the same distinctions throughout all of his work, this study is not concerned with the

[13] B, pp. 226–227.

[14] The literature in these fields is enormous, and I shall simply mention a few better known representative works. Cf. Ludwig Von Bertalanffy, Problems of Life (New York: Harper Torchbooks, 1960) who reviews many of the European versions in the physical, especially biological, sciences; Malinowski, "Culture," in Encyclopedia of The Social Sciences, IV (New York: The Macmillan Co., 1930), pp. 621–645 for an anthropologist's statement; Kurt Koffka, Principles of Gestalt Psychology (New York: Harcourt Brace, 1935); Ernest Nagel, "Wholes Sums and Organic Unities," in Parts and Wholes (New York: The Free Press of Glencoe, 1963), edited by Daniel Lerner, pp. 135–155; Karl W. Deutsch, "Mechanism, Organism, and Society," Philosophy of Science, vol. 18, no. 3, July, 1951, pp. 230–252.

virtues or shortcomings of the organicist conception in itself, however that conception may be construed—as a metaphysics, model, or metaphor.[15] I wish to stress as plainly as possible that my sole interest here is to see what Parsons does with this conception. There are enormous difficulties in his intention as he is well aware. Many different kinds of units and subsystems are involved in his version, quoted above, of the equilibrium of a large scale society. Parsons wishes to develop a theory of the ordering or interdependence of a social system so broad as to embrace every possible variety of social 'subsystem' to be found. Metaphysical arguments can be, and have been, invoked to show in advance the impossibility of such an achievement. But whether flutters of alarm or joy are engendered in a metaphysical bosom at the prospect of such an achievement, a certain forbearance, even fortitude, is in order; for here too, I would insist, the genuine showing of possibility or impossibility in any instance depends upon inspecting the putative achievement itself.

From the first Parsons has insisted that if a social "system is to constitute a persistent order or to undergo an orderly process of developmental change (that is, not disintegrate) certain functional prerequisites must be met."[16] Not until his collaboration with Bales did Parsons' version of these prerequisites become somewhat stabilized. Nevertheless, it is clearly evident in his earlier work that he holds the prerequisites to be of great importance.[17] The prerequisites, in numerous of their formulations, are the major terms in which Parsons cast his thinking on process almost immediately following the publication of *The Structure of Social Action*. And these terms have continued to dominate his thinking on process through his more recent writings on social evolution. Moreover, at certain times in his formulation of them, especially in his work with Bales, and also with Smelser, the conceptual use to which the prerequisites are put begins to resemble a tentative approach to some

[15] Nagel, *ibid.*, suggests that when properties in a system are "interdependent" the system is a functional or organic whole; when "independent" the system is a summative whole. The distinction is not sharp, Nagel declares, and some systems may be both summative and organic.

[16] C, p. 26ff; B, p. 241.

[17] *Cf.* A, p. 6ff; 22, 33ff, 45ff and ch. VIII; B, pp. 24–25, 26, 108, 173, 177, 241; C, pp. 26–36, 115, 167–180.

sort of explanatory statement. They are therefore of primary interest to this study. In his more recent writings Parsons' conceptions are cast in a form corresponding to the form of his earlier writings, although there are some differences in substance to be found in the writings of these periods. To analyze this 'form' and to understand its limitations is the main purpose of this study, as has been mentioned throughout. Now, after these preliminaries, I shall turn first to a brief review of Parsons' new frame of reference fashioned along functionalist lines. This will serve to identify the 'units,' or spheres, of his interest. Of equal importance, the frame of reference should provide a basis for constructing those universal categories necessary for Parsons to be able to overturn the relativism of the historicist viewpoint. This framework is therefore of considerable significance to Parsons' efforts. But for the purpose of a critique of his thinking we will be interested in seeing whether he can establish the logical necessity of this framework itself. For as I have argued earlier, his entire case against the skeptical historicist doctrines will collapse if he cannot produce explanatory statements so linked to this framework that the statements would be impossible to make without the framework. Following an inspection of the new frame of reference, then, I shall turn to his views of equilibrium and interdependence as they apply to certain 'micro-social' domains. In the next chapter, his views shall be examined as they take up the questions of macroscopic application and of the conditions of social evolution.

The Action Frame of Reference and The Equilibrium-Interdependence dence Problem.—In the two books that he published in 1951, *Toward a General Theory of Action* and *The Social System*, Parsons expresses his main interests as follows: (1) to define "the critical subject matter for the theory of action"—which consists of social, personality and cultural systems: (2) to define "the frame of reference of the theory of action (which involves) actors, a situation of action and the orientation of the actor to that situation";[18] and (3) to develop a set of "descriptive categories . . . capable of application to all relevant parts or aspects of a concrete system in a coherent way."[19]

[18] B, p. 55.
[19] C, p. 20.

Let us look a little more closely at the critical subject matter and the frame of reference of the new theory of action, for although they differ in some ways from the corresponding earlier ones outlined in chapter IV, they remain strikingly similar to them in many respects. The theory of action, says Parsons, "is a conceptual scheme for the analysis of the behavior of living organisms . . .

There are four points to be noted in this conceptualization of behavior: (1) Behavior is oriented to the attainment of ends or goals or other anticipated states of affairs. (2) It takes place in situations. (3) It is normatively regulated. (4) It involves expenditure of energy or effort or "motivation" (which may be more or less organized independently of its involvement in action).

"Actions," Parsons continues, "are not empirically discrete but occur in constellations which we call systems. We are concerned with three systems

. . . a *social system* . . . involves a process of interaction between two or more actors . . . the situation toward which the actors are oriented includes other actors. These other actors (alters) are objects of cathexis. Alter's actions are taken cognitively into account as data. Alter's various orientations may be either *goals* to be pursued or *means* for the accomplishment of goals. Alter's orientations may thus be objects for evaluative judgment. There is (in a social system) interdependent and in part concerted action in which the concert is a function of collective goal orientation or *common* values, and of a *consensus* of normative and cognitive expectations.

A personality system. . . (comprises) the interconnections of the actions of an individual actor . . . The Actor's actions are organized by a structure of need dispositions . . . (and) . . . the actions of the single actor have a determinate organization of compatibility or integration with one another. Just as the goals or norms which an actor in a social system will pursue or accept will be affected and limited by those pursued or accepted by the other actors, so the goals and norms involved in a single action of one actor will be affected and limited by one another and by other goals and norms of the same actor.

A cultural system . . . is constituted . . . by the organization of the values,

H

norms and symbols which guide the choices made by actors and which limit the types of interaction which occur among actors ... (It) ... is not an empirical system in the same sense as a personality or social system because it represents a special kind of abstraction of elements from these systems. These elements may exist separately as physical objects and be transmitted from one empirical action system to another . . . In a cultural system the patterns of regulatory norms ... which guide choices of concrete actors ... cannot be made up of random or unrelated elements. If ... a system of culture is to be manifest in the organization of an empirical action system it must have a certain degree of consistency.[20]

The major addition to the "parts" of the system of action with which the earlier means-end scheme was concerned consists of the personality of the actor which is itself a system and an analytical theory "pertinent to the social field." In this conception of action, Parsons is emphatic in his belief that common values and a consensus of normative expectations are most important for the concerted action of the members of a social system. This belief is not inconsistent with his earlier work, and may conceivably be so fashioned as to have explanatory import. But in anything less than the most abstract view, concerted actions are of several different kinds. And as actions are various the less abstractly we think of them, the belief as phrased remains obviously far too vague to be taken as an explanatory statement of any such actions. A refinement of the idea is needed so that we may inspect modalities of actions on the one hand, modalities of values, normative expectations and need dispositions on the other, and then attempt to link all of the sets by deductive propositions, probably of considerable intricacy. We must also, of course, be provided with some justification for the level of abstraction at which any of these modalities is cast—which is to say, we must understand the principle of differentiation that is being employed. Parsons moves precisely to these tasks. The new frame of reference of the theory of action will provide a basis for developing certain cultural, personality, and action modalities—indeed, as we shall see, even for developing a kind of proposition of the relations of these modalities to one another. I shall now outline the new frame of reference with as much brevity as is consonant with

[20] B, pp. 54–55.

accuracy, for we will want to inspect certain claims made of this framework:[21]

1. a. One or more *actors* is involved. An actor is an empirical system of action. The actor is an individual or collectivity...taken as point of reference for analysis of the modes of its orientation and of its processes of action in relation to objects. Action itself is a process of change of state in such empirical systems of action.

b. A *situation* of action is involved. It is that part of the external world which means something to the actor whose behavior is being analyzed... The situation consists of objects of orientation.

c. The *orientation* of the actor to the situation is involved. It is the set of cognitions, cathexes, plans and relevant standards which relates the actor to the situation.

2. The actor is both a system of action and a point of reference. (As the first) the actor may be either an individual or a collectivity. (As the second) the actor may be either an actor-subject...or a social object.

a. The individuality-collectivity distinction: . . . whether the actor is a personality system or a social system.

b. The subject-object distinction:...whether the actor occupies a central position (as point of reference)...or a peripheral position (as object of orientation) for an actor taken as the point of reference...This distinction cross-cuts the individual-collectivity distinction.

3. The situation of action may be divided into a class of social objects (individuals and collectivities) and a class of nonsocial (physical and cultural) objects.

a. *Social objects* (actors as persons or collectivities): . . . The actor-subject may be oriented to himself as an object as well as to other social objects. A collectivity...as a social object, is never constituted by all the action of the participating individual actors...Social objects...may be divided on the basis of (their significance) to the actor-subject as "quality" or "performance" complexes; and they may be divided on the basis of the "scope of their significance" to the actor subject.

(i) The *quality-performance* distinction:...When the actor-subject sees another actor solely in terms of what the actor *is* and irrespective of what that actor does, then we say that actor-object is significant to the

[21] B, pp. 56–60.

subject as a complex of qualities... When the actor-subject sees another actor *solely* in terms of what that actor *does* ... then ... that actor-object is significant ... as a complex of performances.

(ii) The *scope of significance distinction*: (When) social objects... have such broad and undefined significance for the actor-subject that he feels obliged to grant any demand they make of him, so long as the granting ... does not force him to fail in other obligations higher on a priority scale of values ... we (call the significance of the object) *diffuse*. (When) social objects ... have such a narrow and clearly defined significance for the actor-subject that (he) does not feel obliged to grant them anything that is not clearly called for in the definition of the relationship which obtains between them ... (we call the scope of significance of the object) *specific*.

b. Nonsocial objects are ... not actors ... they are physical ... or cultural objects.

(i) *Physical objects* (located in space and time ... do not interact with the actor-subject ... (but are objects only of) ... cognitive, cathectic, and evaluative orientation.) Thus they can constitute instrumentally significant means, conditions, goal objects, obstacles or significant symbols.

(ii) *Cultural objects* are elements in the cultural tradition or heritage... taken as objects of orientation ... These too may be objects of cognitive, cathectic and evaluative orientation in the sense that one may understand the meaning of a law, want a law, decide what to do about a law. Also, these may serve as normative rules, as instrumentally significant means, and as conditions or obstacles of action, or as systems of significant symbols. Cultural objects as norms may be divided into classes (cognitive, appreciative and moral)...

4. The *orientation* of the actor to the situation may be broken down into a set of elements ... (viz.):

a. Motivational orientation: ... those aspects of the actor's orientation to his situation related to actual or potential gratification or deprivation of the actor's need dispositions...

(i) The cognitive mode involves the various processes by which an actor *sees* an object in relation to his system of need-dispostions...

(ii) The cathectic mode involves the various processes by which an actor invests an object with affective significance...

(iii) The evaluative mode involves the various processes by which an actor allocates his energy among the various actions with respect to various cathected objects in an attempt to optimize gratification.

b. *Value orientation*: . . . those aspects of the actor's orientation which commit him to the observance of certain norms, standards, criteria of selection, whenever he is in a contingent situation which allows (and requires) him to make a choice. (There are three such modes of value-orientation, viz.):

(i) The *cognitive* mode . . . involves the various commitments to standards by which the validity of cognitive judgments is established.

(ii) The *appreciative* mode . . . involves commitments to standards by which . . . appropriateness or consistency of the cathexis of an object or class of objects is assessed . . .

(iii) The *moral* mode . . . involves . . . commitments to standards by which certain consequences of particular actions and types of actions may be assessed with respect to their effects upon systems of action . . .

These, then, briefly and barely sketched, are the components of the new frame of reference. They are, of course, a set of definitions some of which are clearer than others—the scope of significance distinction, for example, leaving something to be desired, namely, a distinction. By themselves they explain nothing. The next task Parsons and his collaborators undertake is to identify more precisely what is to be explained. At the very beginning of the discussion of the new frame of reference action was defined as a "change of state . . . in empirical systems of action." Such states must be characterized before they can be explained. As Parsons observes, neither he nor anyone else is yet in a position "to 'catch' the uniformities of dynamic process." However, to place any uniformities that can be 'caught' into a conceptual setting, "and to be in the most advantageous position to extend our dynamic knowledge we must have a 'picture' of the system within which they fit, of the given state of the system and, where changes take place, of what changes into what through what order of intermediate changes."[22]

That 'picture' to which Parsons refers is wrought by the "pattern variable" scheme once prominent in his thought.[23] The pattern variables were intended to be "descriptive" categories for the exhaustive classification of certain "phenomena" found in the three

[22] C, p. 21.
[23] See Parsons' comments in E, ch. III; *cf.* Parsons' essay, "Pattern Variables Revisited: A Response to Robert Dubin," in *American Sociological Review*, August, 1960, vol. 25, No. 4, pp. 467–483.

different systems previously defined. They were to be used to describe, respectively, the role expectations of social systems, the need dispositions of personality systems, and the value orientations of cultural systems. In this way, roles, needs, and values could be compared. Once compared, the kinds of articulations among them for a given system of action at a given time would be noted, and then we would be able to tell when one or another changes, and into what that one does in fact change, and so on.[24] By classifying values, needs, and roles, says Parsons, the pattern variables allow us to take "a first step toward the construction of a dynamic theory of systems of action. To advance toward empirical significance, these classifications will have to be related to the functional problems of on-going systems of action."[25]

All of this seems straightforward enough and consistent with Parsons' scientific aims. We may wonder why the pattern variables are to be exhaustive. And we may wonder why the relation of the classification must be to *functional* problems. But I shall come to Parsons' reasons for the latter relation soon, and offer my own commentary on each wonderment later. We may also begin to feel that the inevitable tedium attendant upon our going through these efforts—certain signs of which are perhaps already noticeable—will be worth it only if there is a successful outcome. But let us brace ourselves and see. We can certainly see why Parsons is concerned to find terms germane to the three different systems of his interest, for he does not wish any one system to be reduced to another. However, it remains unclear why he has selected these and not some other 'basic' terms. Apparently, Parsons believes the phenomena to which such terms as 'kinship' or 'social class' refer, for example, can be analyzed into specific congeries of roles, for he thinks of 'status-role' as being analogous to the particle of mechanics.[26] Indeed, Parsons has endeavored to provide an analysis of kinship structures along the lines of this analogy.[27] However, we shall observe in the following chapter that Parsons does not stress the analogy in his later work.

[24] B, p. 78.
[25] B, p. 93.
[26] C, p. 25.
[27] *Cf.* F.

Parsons does much more than "relate" the classifications of the pattern variables to the functional problems of on-going systems, and we shall understand presently of what this 'much more' consists. Also, the pattern variables are not merely descriptive categories, although they are that too. The pattern variables refer to those things an actor, whether an individual or collection of individuals, prizes, requires, and expects in a given situation. As originally formulated, the pattern variables posed five, basic, exhaustive and universal dilemmas or dichotomies of choice any actor had to resolve before he could orient himself to any situation, "and thus before he can act with respect to that situation."[28] Another way of putting it is this: that before an actor can act in a situation, the meaning of that situation must become clear for him.[29] I am not concerned in this study to contest the proposition that the commonality of values, or of meanings, is some sort of 'condition' important to the persistance of a social action system. I have argued elsewhere that the proposition is misconceived.[30] Here, I would like to call attention to two assumptions Parsons makes whose form is prototypical. The first is that choices must be made before meaning is established. The second is that meaning must be established before action can occur. But notice, also, that granting these, and assuming choices are made and meaning established, it does not follow that action will necessarily occur. Action was defined as a 'process of change of state in an empirical system of action.' The theory of action, Parsons declared, was a scheme 'for the analysis of the behavior of living organisms.' What is the link, if any, between the meaning a situation may have for an actor and that actor's actual behavior in that situation? It is a commonplace of our own experience to have observed people who behave similarly in a situation only to discover later—occasionally to our embarrassment—that some of these people had defined the meaning of that situation quite differently for themselves. Which is hardly to say that meaning is unimportant, but is to say that Parsons conceives the importance of meaning to be as a necessity of

[28] B, p. 77.

[29] Ibid.

[30] "On Davis and Moore Again, or: Dissensus and the Stability of Social Systems," The British Journal of Sociology, December, 1970, vol. XXI, No. 4, pp. 446–454.

action. So here we have an instance of a proposition fashioned by Parsons in the 'a priori' mode: no meaning, no action. However, let us disregard these assumptions and what seems not to follow from them. They will reappear in slightly different terms shortly.

Parsons defines the pattern variables as follows:

1. Affectivity—Affective neutrality
2. Collectivity-orientation—Self-orientation
3. Particularism—Universalism
4. Ascription—Achievement
5. Diffuseness—Specificity

"The first," says Parsons, "concerns the problem of whether or not evaluation is to take place in a situation. The second concerns the primacy of moral standards in an evaluative procedure. The third concerns the relative primacy of cognitive and cathectic standards. The fourth concerns the seeing of objects as quality or performance complexes. The fifth concerns the scope of significance of the object."[31] The immediate source of the distinctions upon which the patterns variables are based is the frame of reference, from whose terms some variables have been culled. At some remove, however, is Tönnies' great work, *Gemeinschaft und Gesellschaft*, which has inspired Parsons to a steady stream of commentary through many of his own works.[32] The Gemeinschaft variables appear on the left side of the listing above, the Gesellschaft on the right. Unlike Tönnies, Parsons does not conceive the variables to constitute merely two typologies significant mainly to different historical periods. Each of the variables, Parsons maintains, is independent of the other. Let us simply accept this and go on. By combining them through cross-tabulation an exhaustive typology of thirty-two possible patterns of orientation are produced, although not all of the patterns occur empirically in human societies.

Parsons has thus achieved here two things. First, he has broken

[31] B, pp. 77–78.
[32] *Cf.* Parsons' "Note on Gemeinschaft and Gesellschaft" in *The Structure of Social Action*, pp. 686–684; see also his commentary on Tönnies in D, pp. 14–15, 130, 360; B, p. 49; C, p. 100. There is an English translation by Charles C. Loomis of Tönnies' work under the title, *Community and Society* (East Lansing, Michigan: Michigan State University Press, 1957).

through the 'fixity' of Tönnies' designations which are equivalent to the fixities of ideal-types. He is therefore in a position to avoid all the dilemmas he believes to accompany such fixities which I reviewed briefly in chapter III: the bias of interpretation, the atomism, the rigid evolutionary scheme, and so on. Second, Parsons is now, presumably, in possession of a small set of universal categories of "meaning" which can span the entire social universe. He has therefore available to him precisely those sorts of categories the historicists lacked, and for whom this lack led, in Parsons' analysis, to the quicksands of epistemological relativism. With these categories in his possession, Parsons is now by his own lights in a position to begin to think of formulating causal explanations. Let us see what he does.

The Functional Problems.—To provide general causal propositions, Parsons must be able to relate the pattern variables to each other in some other way than by mere cross-tabulation. Rules pertaining to the interrelations of roles, values, and needs must be devised so that a variation in any one of these terms will give us, according to the rules, the corresponding variations in each of the others. The pattern variables supply us only with the range of possible variations. The best way to interrelate the variables, Parsons believes, would be achieved by a set of "laws," as in some of the physical sciences, through which "deductive transitions from one aspect or state of a system to another" could be made. Although we are not yet in a position to construct laws, there is a "second best" manner—Parsons' phrase—available that will point the direction to be taken. Structural-functionalism, Parsons says, will allow us to render at least a rudimentary sketch of the relations between roles, values, and needs. So sketched and available to our view, we may one day proceed to a more rigorous conception of their relations.[33]

I have no doubt Parsons means all of this. For among other ideologies to which he may be wedded, there is no question that he is passionately devoted to the positivist model of *explanation,* however strong his reservations are as to the applicability of positivist thought. Functionalism is thus no mere mask contrived to hide, even to himself, the stealthy operation of "political" motives. For

[33] C, ch. I.

we should recognize by now that Parsons also has conceptual 'motives'—purposes is by far the more accurate term—which I have been at some pains to bring out as clearly as possible. When those for whom politics is important fail to recognize the distinction, and give to everything an exclusively political interpretation, politics becomes meaningless—as farcical as any farce, as foolish as any foolishness. Moreover, the question arises for interpretations of this sort in which everything is construed as the sole work of some political motive, whether the argument being advanced is un-wittingly posed as a variant of that very functionalism so despised by its proponents. If this is indeed the case then one must do better than argue against functionalism by recourse to a functional argument.

In Parsons' thinking, at any rate, functionalism is explicitly in-tended to be nothing more than a provisional, 'second best' explan-atory maneuver. Even the second best may turn out to be not good enough for his purposes, but this is rather a different question from the one which inquires into non-conceptual motives. Consider the alternatives open to him. Very briefly: There is the preferred analysis by ways of "laws" which is unfeasible because no laws presently exist. (Or is there anyone who can offer us a sociological law that is not inanely trivial?) There is an 'analysis' of the sort offered by the historicists which, if we accept Parsons' reading, is no analysis at all on the grounds that general categories would be forbidden and that meanings do not exhaust the realities of the social world. There is an analysis by way of 'functions' (not in the mathematical-logical sense) for which there are promising precedents in other 'analytical' fields including the social—for example, some aspects of anthropology and biology. The mere collection of data, however ingenious the techniques by which they are sorted and arranged, amounts simply, we will recall Parsons having said, to "the methodological counterpart of Hume's skepticism in epistemo-logy." And as he has a deep aversion to skepticism—as should we all if we wish to say anything—data collection does not present a genuine analytical alternative. Functionalism, then, for the time being. Reasonable as all this may seem under the circumstances, we will wish to see how well the exercise of this option services his objectives.

In his work with Bales, undertaken shortly after the pattern variable scheme was produced, in form presented above, Parsons identifies the pattern variables with the functional problems themselves, "the two ... turning out to mean essentially the same thing."[34] At a later point he readjusts his opinion on this and argues that the two are not quite the same thing after all. This argument shall be reviewed at the appropriate juncture. For the present, let us glance again at the pattern variables since they have been identified with the functional problems.

The pattern variables are said to be exhaustive as a set of dilemmas. Does this mean the functional problems are also exhaustive? Whether the variables are in fact exhaustive has been questioned by several commentators, but Parsons is adamant: they are exhaustive.[35] I can find no place where he fully explains why this matter is important to him. But we do not have to search far to gain some understanding of his insistence. The exhaustiveness of the pattern variables, in Parsons' view, depends upon three premises: "(1) the acceptance of the basic frame of reference as we have defined it; (2) the acceptance of the level of generality on which we are proceeding ...; (3) the acceptance of our method of derivation through the establishment of primacies among types of interests and the resolution of ambiguities intrinsic to the world of social objects."[36] Assuming we accept all of these, what would be the consequences if the pattern variables are not exhaustive of the range of values, roles, and needs? Either there are more to be found in Parsons' frame of reference, or—and I think this is the heart of the matter—the frame of reference Parsons has developed is too flimsy to provide the unification of the social sciences after which he quests so ardently. And if too flimsy, this must mean other frames of reference from which other 'pattern variables' may be 'derived' have slipped out of the net Parsons has woven. And if there is but one frame of reference

---

[34] E, p. 71.

[35] *Cf.* Max Black's essay, "Some Questions About Parsons' Theories," in *The Social Theories of Talcott Parsons*, edited by Max Black (Englewood Cliffs, New Jersey: Prentice Hall, Inc., 1961), pp. 269–288; see also the review-essay by the late W. J. H. Sprott, "Principia Sociologica," in *The British Journal of Sociology*, September, 1952, vol. III, pp. 203–221.

[36] B, p. 91.

which cannot be integrated with Parsons' frame of reference, the dangers of incommensurability, untranslatibility, relativism and skepticism arise once again. I do not believe it too strong a statement to say that the problem of relativism haunts Parsons, as it has haunted many over the past one hundred years. As I am also perturbed by certain aspects of this problem, my interests and sympathies are somewhat aroused by Parsons' efforts. For anyone else of like mind, this perturbation is no reason to prevent our asking, but all the more reason to ask, whether there are justifiable grounds to reject Parsons' frame of reference—and thus repudiate the claim that he has exhausted the full range of values, needs, and roles. Alas, we will find grounds ...

The conditions of equilibrium, or of order (or of interdependence) are, as we recall, at the same time conceived to be the "condition of the system's being a system." It is Parsons' argument that every system must 'solve' four problems if it is not to disintegrate or if the relationships among its units are not to vary at random. As shall be seen in a moment, Parsons does not conceive of equilibrium merely to be a static state, as has been imputed to his conception by numerous commentators.[37] Perhaps this imputation is a result of a certain density, possibly in Parsons' presentation. Whatever the case may be, Parsons is clear enough that the order of empirical systems "must have a tendency to self-maintenance, which is very generally expressed in the concept of equilibrium. It need not, however, be a static self-maintenance or a stable equilibrium. It may be an ordered process of change—a process following a determinate pattern rather than random variability relative to the starting point. This is called a moving equilibrium, and is well exemplified by growth. Furthermore, equilibrium, even when stable, by no means implies that process is not going on; process is continual even in stable systems, the stabilities residing in the interrelations involved in the process."[38] In what is to follow, Parsons' and Bales's formulations will be presented with reference to the interactions of individuals of small,

[37] See Black's essay, op. cit.; see also the review-essay by G. E. Swanson, "The Approach to a General Theory of Action by Parsons and Shils," *American Sociological Review*, vol. 18, April, 1953, pp. 125–134. There are many others who have made this imputation.

[38] B, p. 107.

experimental, human groups. Of course, Parsons and Bales insist of
these formulations that they are not limited to any particular level of
the study of action "processes from the microscopic to the macroscopic . . . We suggest that the scheme advanced here is in its fundamentals applicable all the way from the phenomena of 'behavior
psychology' on pre-symbolic animal and infantile levels, to the
analysis of the largest scale social systems."[39] However extraordinary
we may think this suggestion to be, we should no longer find it
very surprising. The suggestion is fully congruent with Parsons'
overtly stated intention to construct a unified theory of social science.
In the following chapter we shall look at Parsons' and Smelser's
efforts to carry out a partial macroscopic application of the scheme
of functional problems. But now to the functional problems themselves whose solutions are prerequisite to order. The reader will
observe the points at which the pattern variables are identified.[40]

(1) The problem of *goal attainment* is defined as the gratification
of the units of the system. In pattern variable terms, "when the
culminating activities are about to be carried out, the inhibition on
gratification is suspended and *affectivity* suffuses the goal consum-
mative activity. Similarly, the relation to the object no longer tends
to be universalistic, concerned with realistic prediction of later
effects or relation to other objects. It gives way to a relation of
particularism where the object is a goal object to be possessed,
consumed, enjoyed, or appreciated . . ."[41]

(2) The problem of *adaptation* is defined as the manipulation of
the environment in the interests of goal attainment. In pattern
variable terms, "successful adaptation involves . . . an . . . emphasis
on cognitive orientation . . . the relation of actors to objects needs to
be *universalistic* . . . It is necessary, moreover, if the situation is to be
"mastered" and not simply "accommodated to" for these universal-
istically defined properties to be perceived and dealt with in specific
contexts of relevance to goal interests. Hence the character of the
attitude tends to be marked by *specificity* of interest . . . Finally . . .

[39] E, p. 106; see also p. 175, 192–193, 212.
[40] The definitions of each of the functional problems follows Zelditch's
economic version. *Cf.* Appendix B in F.
[41] E, p. 184. Each of the quotations pertaining to the pattern variables is to
be found in E, pp. 183–185.

where the goal is not yet attained ... it is necessary to inhibit affective or emotional reactions to the objects in order to avoid being drawn off toward other goals ... Hence the attitude tends to be marked by a certain inhibition of *neutrality*."

(3) The problem of *integration* is defined as the attachment of member units to each other as distinct from that which is non-system. In pattern variable terms, "the attitude toward the object is *affectively* toned, and the relation to the object is *particularistic* ... The particularistic attachment to the object, stressing its membership in the same system with ego rather than its specific role or status in the system, involves a whole interrelated constellation of interests held in common ... Hence the character of the attitude is marked by *diffuseness* and the important thing about the object is its *quality*."

(4) The problem of *latency*—or pattern maintenance or tension management—is defined as the continuation of commitment of the member units when they are seen to be systems themselves. Parsons further specifies the meaning of this functional problem as follows: "During periods of suspension of interaction, there exists the imperative, if the system is to be renewed, for the motivational or cultural patterns to be maintained ... To put the matter somewhat differently, a system is confronted by the necessity, as a precondition for its continued existence, of maintaining and renewing the motivational and cultural patterns which are integral to its interaction as a system."[42] In pattern variable terms, "the latent state is 'object oriented' ... the important thing about the object is not what it can do if properly manipulated, but rather what it already does to the emotional state of the actor ... the orientation to the object is primarily in terms of its *quality* ... (there is) a *diffuse* character of the many interests which may be involved ... (and) the internal activity of member units in the latent phase is marked by *neutrality* rather than freely released affect."

In his work with Bales, Parsons maintains the following of the four system problems, or functional prerequisites, listed above: (a) in order for a system to exist in a steady state, it *must* meet the exigencies of action of all four system problems; (b) if the member units are to maintain the boundaries of the system relative to its

[42] E, p. 185.

environment, the system *must* provide an optimum of gratification for the several member units; (c) if the member units are to achieve goal gratification, there *must* be some diversion of motivational energy to the adaptive problems of relation of the system to its environment; (d) if the member units are to maintain the boundaries of the system relative to its environment, there *must* be some diversion of motivational energy to the integrative problems of their mutual solidarity; (e) if the member units are to maintain the boundaries of the system relative to its environment, there *must* be some diversion of motivational energy to the expressive problems of their several tension states.[43]

Notice the many 'musts' of these propositions. They refer to the necessary 'conditions' of a social system. If they are not present in some degree, then a social system is not possible. If a "social system is to constitute a persistent order," Parsons has said, and thus not disintegrate, "certain functional prerequisites must be met." And this is supposed to be the case for any social system, of any kind or size, regardless of age, culture, political arrangement, resources, location in history, the psychological make-up of its members—or any other characteristic one may wish to consider. Any social system, whether in a state of stable or moving equilibrium, must be meeting —that is, somehow solving—at least these system problems. For "the conditions of equilibrium ... are in the last analysis the conditions of a system's being a system." So here we have yet other instances of propositions cast in the "a priori" mode. In fact, I cannot find in Parsons' writings propositions cast in any other mode, but this has yet to be demonstrated. For these instances, it follows, then, that once the necessary 'conditions' of a social system are met, the actual occurrence of that system remains questionable. Therefore, although the propositions may be vindicated, how can the conditions they express be in any analysis 'the conditions of a system's *being* a system'? Should these statements remain puzzling to the reader, I ask him, please, to refer to the discussion of the "A priori in Simmel's Work" in chapter IV, preceding.

---

[43] This again follows Zelditch's economical presentation, F, p. 405; corresponding documentation may be found in E, chapters III and V by Parsons and Bales, the last chapter also with Shils.

It is evident from Parsons' repeated claim of the microscopic-macroscopic range of this functional scheme that he means it to have universal scope.[44] Further, Parsons also states repeatedly that the prerequisites which constitute the set he has formulated exhaust that set.[45] Our suspicions have been borne out. This means that we now have all of the functional prerequisites which are definitely universal. Now we can accumulate empirical findings of other schemes and translate all other schemes into this one. Relativism is thus undone, skepticism banished, and social knowledge can progress on a firm foundation. Or is this so? These issues are hardly settled so quickly and easily.

For even though we may know all of the functional problems any system must solve if it is to exist, maintain itself, and develop in an orderly manner, we do not yet know the conditions, necessary or sufficient, for the solution of *these* problems. One condition is expressed in the well-known phase-orbit notion developed by Parsons, Bales and Shils. I shall reproduce it briefly for the purpose of a few critical comments. First, notice that the "self-collectivity" pattern variable has not been attached to any of the functional problems listed above. This dichotomous variable now refers to "whether the individual actor's orientation in some particular area of activity should be directly constitutive of his solidarity with others in a collectivity, or whether it may remain or become independent of this within certain limits."[46] At yet a later point Parsons interprets this variable "to be a special case of the external-internal" reference, which he defines in much the same way as Homans uses these terms.[47] Parsons' vacillation here is no more than an attempt to clarify his 'frame of reference' and should not, I believe, be seen in any adverse light.

[44] *Cf.* Parsons' comments in "The Point of View of the Author," in *The Social Theories of Talcott Parsons, op. cit.*, p. 327; see also E, p. 102, G, pp. 17–38.

[45] "The Point of View of the Author," *ibid.*

[46] E, p. 67.

[47] Parsons, "General Theory in Sociology," in *Sociology Today*, edited by R. K. Merton, L. Broom, and L. S. Cottrell, Jr. (New York: Basic Books, 1959), pp. 3, 5, 7–37; see Homans, *The Human Group* (New York: Harcourt, Brace and Co., Inc., 1950).

Two main types of activity are related to the preceding four system problems. If activity is represented graphically—which shall not be done here—the four problems may then be defined as the 'poles' of four coördinates. *Instrumental* activity is conceived as the goal attainment and adaptation aspects of the coördinate system, *expressive* activity[48] as the integrative and tension management aspects of the coördinate system. For the graphic representation of activity, a point in action space is defined as the intersection of the coördinates which locate the place of an act. An area in "action space" is then a mass of points. The primacy of one coördinate relative to the other three in the state description of the act or system is referred to as "maximization along a coördinate." The change of the system state from one point to another in successive units of time is called "motion in action space." *A phase* is a "temporal slice" of the action process during which there is a maximization of points in one area in the given time span.[49]

Parsons, Bales, and Shils assume that motivational energy cannot be stored and expended simultaneously. They further assume that when such energy is expended, there will be a single direction of energy expenditure until some diversionary process occurs. This is the so-called principle of inertia Lundberg noted with such high approval.[50] Action by any one actor cannot, on this principle, be maximized along all coördinates, nor along any two coördinates, at the same point in time. However, since a steady state of the system requires that the exigencies of action be met along all four coördinates, prolonged action along any one coördinate places a strain on the system. Therefore, differentiation of action into phases may be derived, given the preceding assumptions, as a necessary condition of the "existence" of the system. Structural differentiation will mean that within any one phase, or at any one point in time, the various units of the system are at different points in the action space, and describe different paths through that space. In each system phase the units are, relative to each other, in different phases,

[48] Parsons later redefines this as "consummatory activity" to avoid certain ambiguities. See "General Theory in Sociology," *loc. cit.*
[49] Again, I follow Zelditch's presentation in F.
[50] See Lundberg's essay, cited in note 20, ch. 1, *supra.*

I

areas, or points. If the direction of structural differentiation is not along all four coördinates, the system will dissolve. Thus, *structural and temporal differentiation are also necessary conditions for the solution of the system problems.*[51]

"The phases we have described," Parsons and his associates say, "are not merely descriptions of different possible states of systems. There are determinate dynamic relations among them, in consequence of the one way flow of motivational energy. There is a general tendency for systems to move towards the G (goal attainment) phase through either the A (adaptive) phase or I (system-integrative) phase ... This model of phase sequence does not however commit us to the contention that no other phase sequence is possible. On the contrary, they (other phase sequences) are in fact most certain ... The empirical order of phases, we assume, is dependent upon the balance and fluctuation of inputs from outside the system as well as internal dynamic interdependencies, and so regular phase movements are in a way a limiting case, dependent upon unusual stability of inputs, a relatively closed system, and a number of other factors (such as) ... the place of the system on the microscopic-macroscopic time range, 'ease of communication' between units in the system, number of units, etc."[52] Conceivably, Parsons and his associates have something resembling a stochastic model in mind when thinking of the empirical order of phases— although this may be rather a fanciful suggestion on my part. Let us look at the two additional necessary conditions for a moment before turning to Parsons' macroscopic applications of the scheme.

Although we have been told the functional problems are exhausted,, these problems, as conditions, obviously do not span the entire range of the necessary conditions of a social system. For we have been given the additional necessities of structural and temporal differentiation. The first question that must immediately arise is whether these new conditions can be 'derived' from Parsons' frame of

[51] In another essay published in 1953, coinciding in time with his collaboration with Bales, Parsons states that "the theory of stratification *is* general sociological theory pulled together with reference to a certain fundamental aspect of social systems." *Cf.* "A Revised Analytical Approach to the Theory of Social Stratification," in D, p. 439.

[52] E, pp. 187–188.

reference or integrated with that framework in some way. If not, the framework is simply inadequate to the unification of the social sciences for which it is intended, and the relativistic problems remain, presumably, unsolved. The second question that may be asked is suggested largely, although not completely, by the first. Are there yet other conditions possible and, if we cannot be sure these other conditions have been exhausted, can we be sure Parsons' framework is adequate to their 'derivation'? Several commentators have observed that Parsons everywhere seeks to conceptualize the social system "as a whole," thus producing a "grand theory" to which one or another commentator has pejoratively imputed a 'metaphysical interest,' a 'theoretical conceit,' or what not. We do not have to resort to what I consider dubious imputations of this kind to understand why Parsons believes he must proceed in this fashion—whatever the merit of such imputations may be. If Parsons cannot bring out all of the conditions necessary to a social system and conceptually interweave these conditions with his framework, the epistemological status of his framework will remain undecided. Given his formulation of the problems, epistemological and scientific, this is not all he must do, but he must certainly do this as well.

To the first question: One of the difficulties in seeing the relationships of various parts of Parsons' work to each other comes, I think, from his usage of the term 'derive.' He does not only mean 'deduce' by that term but also something like 'by formal analogy' or 'by metaphorical extension." Structural and temporal differentiations are 'derived' as necessary conditions of system stability *given* the 'principle of inertia' *and* the four 'system problems.' Here the usage of 'derive' comes closest in meaning to 'deduce,' the givens forming premises, the necessary conditions a conclusion. The pattern variables are 'derived' from the frame of reference. In this usage the meaning of 'derive' is far less clear. If the reader will check back, he will find that certain of the terms in which the pattern variables are cast have been mentioned in the frame of reference, under items 3.a.i, 3.a.ii, and 4.a.ii. Parsons has said, we will remember, that the method of derivation of the pattern variables "consists in the establishment of primacies (of choice) among types of interests and the resolutions of ambiguities intrinsic to the world of social objects." The primacies of choice are scattered throughout the frame of reference. As there seems to be a classificatory operation involved here, I suggest the meaning of 'derive' in this instance would be closer to 'by formal analogy' rather than to strict logical 'deduction.' The fact that the distinctions of the pattern variable scheme are analogous to the distinctions drawn by Tönnies is not pertinent to the question of derivation of the pattern variables from the frame of reference itself. Part of my reason for reproducing the frame of reference so extensively (though not nearly with the extensiveness of the original) is to allow the reader to evaluate my own comments on the meaning of 'derivation' and come to some decision on this matter for himself.

What now of the 'principle of inertia'? Consider the statements: (1) 'motivational energy cannot be stored and expended simultaneously'; and (2) 'energy expenditure will be in a one-way direction until diverted.' So far as I can make out, neither of these statements can be logically deduced from any combination of items in the frame of reference. There are, perhaps, items within the frame of reference remotely analogous to these statements. Parsons does say, under 4.a.iii. that motivational energy is allocated, implying a scarcity of such energy to begin with. The two statements, although seemingly not deducible from the frame of reference, do not appear contradictory of any of that framework's formulations. (Perhaps they are 'metaphorical extensions' of the idea of a scarcity of energy?) Whatever the case may be, and from wherever they may have come, so long as the two statements can be integrated with Parsons' framework without undue alteration of the framework, nothing is yet taken from him. But this is the juncture where a difficulty arises. Will the integration of these two statements and therewith the two, new necessary conditions require some slight modification of the framework? Parsons is perfectly aware of this difficulty and of what it may forebode. For whether these statements are 'metaphorical extensions' or not, the scarcity of motivational energy implied in 4.a.iii. could as well refer to the allocation of various quantities of energy in several directions simultaneously. This simultaneity of directions, however, is ruled out by the principle of inertia. Therefore, something is needed to 'derive' the limited, *exclusive*, one-way direction of energy expenditure stated in the principle. Parsons believes the inertia principle to be somehow involved with those primacies of choice which allowed the pattern variable scheme to be 'derived.' At times he says the inertia principle, and the statement preceding it, are "manifestations of," or "analogous to," the postulates along which the pattern variables are composed.[53] Perhaps he means something like this: At a given time, choices can be only one of a kind (particularism *or* universalism; specificity *or* diffuseness, etc.). If one does not choose, one cannot act. If one acts, energy is expended. At a given time, when one acts energy is expended 'in the direction' of the kind of choice made. This is the closest I can come to 'deriving' the inertia principle swiftly, but with slight expenditure of energy and rather less than Euclidean rigor. It is not certain whether the major premise is 'in' the frame of reference or has already been derived from it in some way. Nor does the conclusion seem exactly equivalent to the inertia principle. Furthermore, the statement 'motivational energy cannot be stored and expended simultaneously' remains yet to be derived. I invite the reader to try his hand at it. Functionalism may be 'second best' and derivations may be of several different kinds. But in this issue of pressing importance to him Parsons should, and does, want to be able to show in the strongest possible terms that his framework retains stability. The strongest terms are those shorn of as many ambiguities as possible; they are logical terms.

I think the question of whether Parsons' framework will have to be modified to accommodate the principle of inertia and all the rest is not easily decided. Even certain minor modifications would give rise to severe doubts. For to the extent the framework is modified by additions not logically related to it, the framework would not possess quite the breadth or stability Parsons desires of it. But to the extent the modifications do not contradict the basic terms of the framework, these terms would not be abandoned although their number would now be increased. Logicians have undermined various thought systems for less. Certainly the new framework is modified, and many new, logically unrelated categories added, in comparison to the early means-end schema. For this reason, the

[53] E, ch. V.

means-end schema is *not* that 'non relative' point of reference which would allow all other analytical theories of groups to be translated into it—as Parsons wanted the means-end schema to be. But as to the new framework itself in the present situation, the question of *its* modification seems decidable only through a complex logical procedure. As I wish to go on to issues of greater interest, let me put the question in the best light and assume the framework will be found stable upon the most careful logical scrutiny—at least for the time being.

However, even in this light Parsons seems to have opened an abyss. He must now begin a search for all of the necessary, universal conditions of a social system that are possible, and he must somehow be able to tell when he has exhausted these conditions. Then, he must be able to show these conditions are unthinkable without his framework. Further, he must also produce sufficient conditions, explanations, of all the 'objects'—the units and systems—of his concern, and show that these explanations are also unthinkable without his framework. And he must be able to do all of these without adding 'underived' basic categories to his framework, or else the entire point of the framework will be lost. I am somewhat hesitant under the circumstances to raise the question of vindicating all the conditional propositions which loom, but this question must be faced too, with all of the others.

In his *Logic* Hegel ventured a criticism of Kant's thought as follows: Kant, Hegel said, in answer to the question, 'What does the world rest on?'—offers us an elephant. (The a priori categories). In answer to the question, 'But what does the elephant rest on?'— Kant gives us a tortoise. Now if we were to ask Kant what the tortoise rests on, he will, no doubt, come forth with some other mythological beast, and so on and on without end. Is Parsons' present situation analagous to Kant's? Perhaps we will find an answer to this question when we look at the macroscopic applications of his scheme.

CHAPTER SEVEN

Of Thinking and Explaining the Composition of Large Scale Societies and Their Evolution

As Parsons' work progresses the philosophical themes give way and the scientific themes become increasingly dominant. However, the philosophical themes never completely disappear. They are sounded again and again, fleetingly, to remind his readers that his work is indeed a body of work in which all of the themes, philosophical and scientific, are related as though in a counterpoint. I shall call attention to the places at which the philosophical themes reappear to help support the interpretation of Parsons' work that is being advanced in this study.

So far, we have found all of Parsons' scientific propositions to be concentrated upon the conditions presumed to be necessary and universal to any social system. No longer does he say outright, as he did in his 1937 work, that his framework is logically necessary to all social knowledge. But he is unflagging in his zeal to unify all the social sciences and to make apparently disparate social theories commensurable. A measure that will be common to all social theories is equivalent to a "non-relative point" upon which all social theories may be affixed. The logic of verification is one such point. If one cannot think without certain categories, these categories are obviously other such non-relative points. Parsons' philosophical interests have thus not subsided.

But now to the functional scheme, "identical" to the pattern variables which have been derived, let us grant, from that non-relative framework of categories logically necessary to social knowledge which he had developed with Shils. The functional scheme has been laid out sufficiently, I will assume, so that the reader will be able to follow the discussion with minimal reference to the ingredients of that scheme. Parsons and Bales directed their efforts to interpreting the activities of "small social systems"—groups consisting of approximately twenty people. I do not believe they have vindicated any of their propositions as to these activities, although their interpretations render these activities intelligibly for us. I shall discuss the matter of vindication soon. For the moment, let us consider Parsons' interpretations of the actions of 'large social systems' consisting of millions of people.

In his later work with Smelser, Parsons' concern is to outline the (possible?) ways the solutions of the functional problems are allocated throughout an entire society. It is not of paramount importance here to look at every detail of his conceptualization although some broad aspects may be noted. A society is composed of sub-systems which are systems in their own right. The functional problems of a society must be solved for that society to persist, as is true for every one of the 'sub-systems' within it. The economy, for example, as a system, is faced with the exigencies of any system. However, as a sub-system within the larger society, the economy's main function is to contribute to a solution of the larger society's *adaptive* problems. Generally, the economy produces wealth and income, each of which may be considered as "means to attain any goals valued by the system or its sub-units."[1] However, wealth and income, as they are ordinarily conceived, are not the only "means." Educational and defense institutions, for example, as they too produce 'means' of sorts, may also be placed within the economic sector. The polity, on the other hand, functions to attain *system goals*—not merely to produce means for such attainment. The primary function of the polity is to "maximize the *capacity* of the society to attain its system goals, i.e., collective goals." But of what does this capacity consist? "Power (in fact) is the capacity to mobilize the resources of the society, including wealth and other ingredients such as loyalties, 'political responsibility,' etc. to attain particular and more or less immediate collective goals of the system."[2] Therefore, in Parsons' view, the polity is not merely the 'government,' although many

[1] I will continue to cite Parsons' works alphabetically, as in the preceding chapter, *cf.* note 5. G, p. 21.
[2] G, p. 41.

governmental activities are included within the polity. The polity also includes banking and finance systems and yet other 'systems' as well. The sub-systems which function to integrate and maintain the patterns of the larger society are not identified by Parsons in apposite terms. However, state and church may be placed among the integrative, the family among the pattern maintaining, sub-systems. Whether the sub-systems are indeed sub-*systems* or mere classificatory rubrics is not clear from Parsons' discussion. Whatever the case, Parsons attempts schematically to trace some of the inter-changes between the various 'sub-systems' in the larger society, and to give some idea of how these inputs and outputs, as he phrases these interchanges, may be conceived to contribute to the solution of one or more of the functional problems of the larger society, and of the sub-systems as well.[3]

Parsons still holds to the notion that there are 'functional problems' whose solutions are necessary for the existence and maintenance of any society. From the foregoing, it is equally apparent that structural differentiation is also held to be necessary as a condition for the solution of the functional problems. The question of temporal differentiation is obscure in this analysis, possibly because the defini-tion of the units involved has undergone some change. In his earlier work with Bales, the "concrete" members of the small groups under observation were considered to be the 'units' composing those groups. The member-units, who could be treated as systems in their own right with the appropriate shift of reference, were observed to become differentiated 'structurally' and 'temporally' throughout the intervals of their interaction. No one could foretell whether these differentiations would occur, but their occurrence was believed necessary to the completion of group tasks and the achievement and maintenance of group stability. However, in Parsons' work with Smelser the units involved are no longer unambiguously "concrete." The sub-systems taken to be the "units" of the larger society now consist of the polity, the economy, etc. There are, apparently, only *four* such units of the larger society corresponding in their activity to a solution of the four functional problems. "An economy," says Parsons, "... is a special type of social system. It is a functional

[3] *Cf.* ch. IV, G.

sub-system of the more inclusive society, differentiated from other sub-systems by specialization in the society's adaptive function. It is one of four sub-systems differentiated on a cognate basis and must be distinguished from each of the others. It must also be distinguished from all concrete collectivities which, whatever their functional primacy, are *always* multifunctional."[4]

For all the apparent simplicity and suggestiveness[5] achieved by identifying the units of the larger society with the functional sub-systems, I think the functional scheme itself is now beclouded. The suggestiveness consists, first, in the fact that the concept of the social, or of society, is presently composed of the concepts of all four 'system problems' taken together and recast as sub-systems themselves. To borrow a recent formula of Althusser's, Parsons has again produced the theoretical constitution of the "social object"—but here in a concise, streamlined fashion.[6] Second, each sub-system will, presumably, be seen to produce a specific medium necessary for the existence and maintenance of the larger society. And third, all of the media—if they are somewhat analogous to the 'wealth and income' produced by the economy—will be construed to vary either in degree or kind. By combining degrees or kinds of all the media, we may be able to approach an understanding of 'concrete' societal modalities, and so gain some access to the historical world now shorn of all relativistic impediments. There is a parallel to the pattern variable scheme.

However, none of this is presently possible. For the obscurity of the scheme lies in the fact that the relations between sub-systems (or the 'media' they produce) are conceived to be made-up of 'inputs' and 'outputs.' To be able to chart such interchanges requires, at the barest minimum, that the media and their variations be perfectly well understood. The trouble is that the media 'produced' by two of the sub-systems are *conceptually* unclear at the macroscopic range. (Let us assume the others—wealth and power—are pellucid). The vagueness of Parsons' present formulation does not merely involve

[4] G, p. 306.

[5] *Cf.* Leslie Sklair, "The Fate of the 'functional requisites' in Parsonian Sociology," *British Journal of Sociology*, vol. xxi, #1, March, 1970, pp. 30–42.

[6] *Cf.* Althusser, *Reading Capital* (with Etienne Balibar) (London: New Left Books, 1970), chs. 6 and 7.

the imperfect "fit between system problems and institutions"—
as one of his sympathetic critics has observed.[7] To cite this point as
an imperfection is perhaps to harken back to Parsons' general idea
of units and systems which, as the idea is supposed to apply to
everything, does not distinguish any particular system. I believe the
question now is to clarify the media 'produced' by the integrating
and pattern maintaining sub-systems that are appropriate to a large
society.

In *Economy and Society* Parsons elaborates the adaptation imperative as a sub-system so that the functioning of this sub-system will
be clearer to us in the societal reference. If a society does not have
resources, it cannot adapt itself to any exigencies. Later, he also
undertakes further efforts to pitch the 'medium' of the goal attaining
sub-system to the societal level.[8] If resources such as money, materiel,
knowledge, property, and so on are not mobilized, a society cannot
reach any goals. 'Power'—or access to resources—is the mobilizing
medium. Following Parsons, I put these propositions in non-
quantitative terms. But he is hopeful that a "scale" for each of the
major terms can be devised. If we will remember, the functional
scheme is to have a microscopic-macroscopic range. Notice, however, that to understand how any of the functional imperatives are
met by a person, say, or by some animal, will not bring us instantly
to an understanding of how the imperatives are 'solved,' and in
what their solution consists, either for a small group or a large
society. The point of reference is not shifted with the greatest of ease.
We must wonder whether this fact portends unbridgeable difficulties
in the accurate 'translation of one scheme into another' ...

The economy (production of means) and the polity (mobilization
of resources, or power) are two sub-systems of a large society
differentiated 'on a cognate basis.' An oversimplified way of striking
the distinction that may be of aid is this: some people make tools,
some people use tools. Now Parsons must turn his attention to the
'media' of the integrating and pattern maintaining sub-systems of
a large society. Here his interest will be to conceive those media

[7] See Devereux's essay, cited in note 17, ch. I, *supra.*, esp. p. 61.
[8] *Cf.* Parsons, *Sociological Theory and Modern Society* (New York: Free
Press, 1967), ch. 10.

which, so to speak, direct people in the cooperative and in the proper use of tools. His discussions are again fertile, although marked by some indecision in outcome. I will omit the details and go to the firmest, most recent statement of his reflections, for I wish to be able to raise a few questions pertaining to 'vindication' that will follow.

Over the span of a decade, and in several essays—the most recent appearing in 1968—Parsons suggests that the integrating and pattern maintaining 'media' of a society may be conceived, respectively, as "influence" and "value commitment."[9] To say that someone is influenced is to say that he has heeded an appeal to some kind of action. Thus, if all appeals to any kind of action are ignored, not even two of the members of a society in which such appeals have been made can be solidary, and their concerted action cannot occur. Parsons defines 'solidarity' here similarly to Durkheim. To say that someone is committed to a value is to say that he has both capacity and promise to bring into existence a particular idea of what is 'desirable.' As we would expect to see, and will see more fully in later discussion, Parsons believes value commitments to have a special place in the relations among all the societal sub-systems of action. For any society, then, if there is no *regulation* of what is considered to be a desirable:

(a) level of *utility* of goods and services available to the economy and to the larger society for consumption,
(b) level of *effectiveness* of power by which societal goals are attained,
(c) level of kind of *solidarity* of the various member-units of the society,
(d) level or kind of '*integrity*' and '*flexibility*' of the standards of choice (patterns of value) distributed throughout the society,

there can be no economic solvency, no success in mobilizing resources, no consensus among societal members, no consistency of value pattern—everything will vary 'at random'—and thus the society will disintegrate. Parsons does not express preference for any one version of the desirable, or for any degree to which the desirable may be regulated. Certain members of the ideological delegation should be reminded that he has elicited thirty-two general terms in

---

[9] See Parsons, *ibid.*, ch. 11, also Parsons' essay "On The Concept of Value Commitments," *Sociological Inquiry*, vol. 35, #2, Spring, 1968, pp. 135–159.

which different orientations to the 'desirable' may be put. We shall look at his final emendations of the pattern variables later.

All of the above sounds familiar if slightly homiletic. There are similarities here to Parsons' early means-end scheme, but there is now perhaps greater scientific promise. Parsons attempts to bring out a few of the general "mechanisms" by which any kind or degree of value commitment, say, may be established. Terms such as compliance, sanctions, and socialization designate the mechanisms. His remarks are suggestive but of no pertinence to this study. For although the mechanisms point to the interrelations of the media, they do not yet tell us of any of the determinate covariations that may occur between them. What is pertinent to this study, however, is Parsons' notion of "interchanges" between the media of the societal sub-systems. Will a variation in kind or degree of any one medium lead to variations in kind or degree of all the others? Can anyone even begin to propose what some of these interdependencies will be? Parsons has pursued the answers to these sorts of questions all of his intellectual life. If the reader will bear with me, I shall attempt to provide in a few dogmatic strokes a rough gauge of the distance yet to be traversed, and of one or two features of the terrain to be encountered, before the merest answers to these questions may be overtaken.

On Vindication.—To dispel the slightest possibility of misunderstanding: I do not intend to invoke any empiricist credo in discussing the matter on hand. The issues I wish to raise are entirely conceptual in character: In any event, I believe eye and mind are inseparable, and that "concrete objects" cannot be sought by induction or any other way without their concepts. This statement may be contested —it denies, for example, that there is ever a pure "sensuous grasp" of objects—but I shall not defend it here as I wish to meet Parsons as reliably as possible on his own grounds.

Consider the "media." They are concepts intended to differentiate the 'concrete forms' through which the functional imperatives may be met. However, the media as defined are not to be taken for the concepts of the concrete objects themselves. The 'real forms' of the media—defined, say, by the concept of 'money' produced by the sub-system of the economy—are conceived to circulate throughout an entire society. Varying extents of such circulation, and varying quantities of things circulated, are presumed to have some effect upon the character of the society. Furthermore, whatever is included under the value commitment medium is held to play some "governing" role upon the other media—although this role is neither iron-clad nor well defined. Parsons believes the circulation of those things the concepts of the media are supposed to distinguish may be understood in analogy to a 'cybernetic system.' We shall glance again at his version of this analogy later. Although the value commitment medium may 'govern' the other media, particular extents and quantities of everything included under the remaining media will have some effect upon the degree to which value commitments do indeed "govern." All of this suggests that Parsons wishes to move towards statements explanatory in form.

The first and most apparent difficulty to be noted is that the definitions of the media are ambiguous. Parsons is altogether aware that there is a major difficulty in defining the 'boundaries' of the functional sub-systems.[10] What is indeed to be included under the economy? Anything that produces a resource. But are resources defined uniformly, or can we snare every definition of a resource even for a given moment? There are difficulties of at least equal magnitude in defining the media pertinent to each of the sub-systems. A tool is something that can be known only in its use. Can we always tell when something is being 'used'? When one acts he has heeded a call to action. Which call? These are not niggling questions, as Parsons is fully cognizant, for we often have trouble interpreting these questions in situations familiar to us. In situations remote from us the dilemmas of interpretation become formidable. Until we gain greater conceptual clarity of the 'media,' the so-called interchanges between the sub-systems will remain vague. The first conceptual difficulties to be overcome, then, are those of definition: the societal sub-systems and the media that pertain to them must be rendered more exactly. If these tasks can ever be discharged, they remain to be discharged in the future.

However, as we shall see, Parsons attempts through his evolutionary scheme to suggest modalities of certain of the functional

[10] Parsons, *ibid.*, p. 149.

sub-systems. Just as he had worked out modes of orientation in the pattern variables, so he also attempts, but now very tentatively, to point to modes of economy, polity, solidarity and regulation of the 'desirable.' For, as all the sub-systems are supposed to be the elements of any society, the modalities of these elements, and their several combinations, will give us the variations of society that have existed throughout history. It is not without interest to note that Louis Althusser, the French Marxist, defines certain of the theoretical tasks of structuralist Marxism in similar ways—a fact to which George Lichtheim has been among the first to call attention.[11] Indeed, a few of the *Marxist* criticisms of Althusser resemble certain of the criticisms that have been aimed at Parsons—the "a-historicism" of outlook, the so-called "Platonism" of the conceptual apparatus being employed, etc.[12] If Marxism is not merely historicism, in any of the senses of that term discussed previously, Parsons' epistemological enterprise is not nearly so anti-Marxist as has been made out. However interesting, I find no particular comfort to be gained from this fact.

Assuming the definitional quandaries have been resolved, the question of the relations of the elements—the interplay between the sub-systems—remains open. Suppose, as Parsons wants, "scales" can be constructed so that we can tell at some moment the full quantity of the media available to a given society. (The reader may be reminded that 'gross national product' does not exhaust the economic medium, and also be assured I am aware of having entered an imaginary realm which may not be distinguishable from fantasy). All the media are supposed to "circulate." But as they do circulate, and a medium of a certain degree enters one sub-system as an "input," we have no idea of the degree to which that medium will emerge from the sub-system in question as a new "output" on the way to yet other sub-systems, and so on. If one sub-system gains full possession of any one medium, the society will then collapse. But a mere 'empirical' tracing of the quantities of a medium as it enters and then leaves one sub-system en route to the

---

[11] *Cf.* citation in note 3, ch. I, *supra*.

[12] *Cf.* Gouldner, cited in note 10, ch. I, *supra*; also *cf.* Alistair Davidson, "Althusser: Marxism Old and New," *Arena*, #19, August, 1969.

next will tell us only that a variation in degree of the medium will or will not have occurred in passage. We should want to know when such variations do or do not occur and what effects this may have upon the other sub-systems. And we should want to know what the covariations in the quantities of the media will be, or would have been, as the media circulate among the sub-systems of the society. An empirical reckoning cannot answer these questions for us. Only a theory of the relations of the modes of the elements can begin to approach answers to the questions Parsons has himself asked. To conceive modalities of each of the sub-systems will allow, let us assume, for the possible range of their combinations to be "wrought"—as in the pattern variable scheme. Even if we have all of the sub-system modalities, however, there remains the question of the relations of the sub-systems. Are these combinations of sub-systems possible to conceive but 'empirically' empty? What are the "rules" which relate one modality of sub-system to another, and which make certain combinations 'empty' and others 'real'? Parsons' provisional answer, as shall be seen, is that certain modalities of sub-systems are necessary for certain modalities of others under certain conditions. This is the beginning of a 'functional' answer— tentative, suggestive, 'second best.' But the answer does not yet permit us to 'deduce' the covariations in quantities of the media for any moment of *any* given society; there are too many unknowns and too many vaguely knowns. Deductions of this sort may seem an impossibly difficult requirement to fulfill. And yet this is the very requirement Parsons has imposed upon himself before "verification" of a theory can be undertaken. His comments on this matter have been reproduced in the last few pages of chapter II, above.

Parsons' functional and 'cybernetic' notions are insufficiently developed to pose the questions of their 'scientific vindication.' But are they not suggestive and provocative notions, and have they not proved fruitful in his work with Bales? And do not these qualities provide some justification for the continued effort to develop these notions? I think the notions may be fruitful although I am uncertain of the extent of their fertility and whether the form in which they have been put is even accurate at the microscopic range. With the understanding that I am not expert at small-group research, and that I rely solely on Parsons' and Bales's accounts, I venture the following logical observations of their analysis. Briefly, (1) Parsons and Bales selected 'normal' people to compose a possible group. (2) These people were given various instructions and then placed in a small-group laboratory. (3) The experimentors noted that among the subjects a two-fold direction of activity ensued: one set of activities was directed towards achieving group stability ("solving the system problems"), another towards completing the 'group task.' An ordered sequence of phase movements was also discerned: activity proceeded from a relative emphasis on the 'problems' and 'solutions' of orientation, thence to evaluation, control, decision, and finally to tension reduction.[13] The 'solution of the system problems' through differentiation of the activities of the members of the group (in phases) was claimed to be *necessary* for the achievement and maintenance of group stability. Parsons' and Bales's interpretation has given us an intelligible account of the activities of these experimental groups.

Does it not follow, however, that if any one of the 'system problems' was made impossible to solve, the group would not have been able to achieve and maintain stability? *Solutions* to the 'system problems,' in this setting, have been conceived necessary as "conditions." But so far as I can tell, the experimental manipulation of *any* of the so-called *conditions* necessary to group stability never took place, for the idea of functional exigencies was treated as unproblematic. Perhaps the technical difficulties of experimental manipulation of any of these conditions are insuperable—even in a situation where empirical and operational implements are in full force! Whatever the case may be, not manipulating the 'necessary conditions' in the experimental setting leaves the question of their "necessity" unsettled. For in the simplest case: either one of the conditions is not necessary, or not necessary for all members, as a condition for the existence of a small group. If one of the conditions

[13] In addition to *Working Papers in the Theory of Action* (E), see also Robert Bales, *Interaction Process Analysis* (Cambridge: Addison-Wesley Press, Inc., 1951) and R. Bales with F. Strodbeck, "Phases in Group Problem Solving," *Group Dynamics*, edited by D. Cartwright and A. Zander (Evanston: Row, Peterson & Co., 1953), ch. 26.

K

is not necessary for some groups, then the universality of the condition may not be claimed. If one of the conditions is not necessary for some group members, but necessary for others, the condition must be reconceptualized. Some commentators have *suggested* that group loyalty, for example, is either not necessary for some groups, or not necessary for all members, as a condition for the existence of certain kinds of groups.[14]

Pending the empirical adjudication of these propositions—if that is ever possible—no one of them is in a favored position. Assuming the decision will favor Parsons, he will have told us something of group life, but he will not yet have told us everything that he wishes: for he will not yet have explained group life "causally." We have already seen that this lack, on the basis of his own hopes and standards, places his action framework in a vulnerable position. But is the position of the action framework thus especially vulnerable? If the standard to be applied is that of causal explanation in the "covering law" sense, the action framework is no better than other sociological frameworks for which there are aspirations to universality. From which general 'framework' can we find an 'adequate explanation' of any 'social facts'? Not being better than other general frameworks, however, it does not follow that the action framework is any the worse. Putting the question of causal explanation in abeyance, there are yet other grounds on which all general frameworks presently available to us may be judged equally deficient. I shall discuss this matter in the following chapter.

The Final Frame of Reference, The Pattern Variables, The Functional Problems.—When Parsons turns his attention to deciphering modalities of societal sub-systems, and thus modalities of society, he raises the question of the varying conditions and requirements of societal adaptation. This question leads him to altering the framework which once 'fused' the pattern variables to the functional requisites. The new, and now apparently stabilized framework, includes *four* systems involved in the larger system of social action. Parsons dubs these systems the "organism," the "personality," the

14 *Cf.* Gouldner, "Reciprocity and Autonomy," *op. cit.*; also David Lockwood, "Some Remarks on the Social System," *British Journal of Sociology,* June, 1956, #7, pp. 134–135.

"social system," and the "cultural system."[15] By comparison to the 1950 framework, cited in chapter VI, the 1960's version of the action framework has aggrandized unto itself a new 'system,' the organism. Again, Parsons raises the questions of how each of these terms may be defined as a 'system,' and how all of these systems are organized when taken together. Parsons' conceptions here do not correspond in every point to any of his earlier formulations of 1937 or 1950. But his concerns are here much the same as his earlier ones, and he also makes many of the same claims that he made of his previous frameworks:[16]

... the study of human social behavior *necessarily* involves a frame of reference here called "action" . . . Essentially, it means a type of theoretical scheme incompatible with the form of "reductionism" characteristic of a great deal of our earlier scientific tradition. Action treats behavior as "goal-directed," as "adaptive," as "motivated," and as guided by symbolic processes . . . The behavioristic position was a major example of reductionism and tended to deny the scientific legitimacy of all "subjective" categories, of all concepts of "meaning." As in the battles over the status of science itself and over empiricism in this area, it can be said that the fight is over. Sociological theory today is clearly couched in terms of motives, goals, symbols, meanings, means and ends, and the like.

Thus the philosophical themes reappear again.

The fact that Parsons' claims of each of his frameworks remain substantially the same, although the frameworks alter, may give rise to the suspicion that none of the claims is warranted in any instance. Is Parsons being overeager in his zeal, and does he leap too quickly to the assertion of his claims? Yet notice that each new framework does not discard the preceding one entirely, but incorporates all of the 'old' systems and 'adds' them to new systems. I shall take the line, in order to proceed, that almost no framework issues fully formed, however great the flash of inspiration may be, and that time is needed in order to think through the implications of what one is

[15] These distinctions appeared in several publications by Parsons occurring in close sequence. Material here is drawn from the "Pattern Variables Revisited" essay, *op. cit.*, some of Parsons' comments in H and I, and in "The Point of View of the Author" essay in Black's volume, *op. cit.*

[16] H, vol. 1, pp. 32–33.

after. Reasonable though this cliché sounds, I think it is even correct. Parsons has always been impervious to the doubtful charms of reductionism. Of the early means-end scheme Parsons had also said that "it is impossible even to talk about action in terms that do not involve a means-end relationship." But if now "organism," "personality," etc. *must* be included in the system of action, one may wonder whether all systems relevant to human social behavior have been finally assembled. This question arises from the presently visible prospect that human social behavior is not perfectly closed and self-contained as is, say, a human language whose structure remains firm despite dialect and regional differences (according to Chomsky). Further thought may yet find other "necessary" systems to be included in a determinate theory of social action.

However, Parsons now says that "the basic sub-systems of the general system of action constitute a *hierarchial* series of agencies of control of the behavior of individuals or organisms. The behavioral organism is the point of articulation of the system of action with the anatomical-physiological features of the physical organism and is its point of contact with the physical environment. The personality system is, in turn, a system of control over the behavioral organism; the social system, over the personalities of its participating members; and the cultural system, a system of control relative to action systems."[17]

The 'control' of each of these systems, Parsons believes, "is that of normative control (in the cybernetic sense), or the control by a more highly *organized* entity over one which is less highly organized, which stands in a 'conditional' relation to the former."[18] In which respect is the cultural system at the apex of the 'hierarchy of control'? What does 'control' mean? The answers Parsons wishes to give to these questions are suggested by his new framework which distinguishes the 'functional imperatives' from the pattern variables.[19] I will not recapitulate this framework as extensively as the earlier, except to note the differences between them.

Parsons declares that there are two sets of "problems" every

---

[17] H, p. 38.
[18] "The Point of View of the Author," *op. cit.*, p. 324.
[19] "Pattern Variables Revisited," *op. cit.*, p. 468ff.

action system must face simultaneously. One set is 'internal,' and concerns the question of how the system is able to keep its own parts in *some* definite relation. This is the "problem of order," or of system maintenance. Again, Parsons is not concerned with the establishing of a particular kind of order, but with those things necessary for any kind of order to be established. The functional imperatives apply to the internal reference. The other set of problems is external, and concerns the question of how any action system is enabled to adapt to the "environment," or anything that is not itself, and yet maintain itself as a system. The requirements of such adaptation are as follows:

1. In order to symbolize the *adaptive* significance of objects in the environment of an action system (i.e., to "understand" them cognitively), it is necessary to categorize them in terms of what actually or potentially they "do" (performance), *and* to orient to them with affective neutrality . . .

2. In order to symbolize (the goal attainment significance of) objects that are external to the system . . . it is necessary to focus their possible meaning on specific bases of interest or "motivation" (specificity), *and* on their potential "belongingness" in a system of meanings which also defines the system of action (particularism) . . .

3. In order to symbolize . . . the significance of *norms* that are external to the system, it is necessary to treat them as aspects of an objectively "given" state of affairs or "order" (quality), *and* to treat them with affectivity . . .

4. In order to symbolize . . . the significance of "sources of normative authority," it is necessary to combine a universalistic definition of the object, as having properties not dependent on its inclusion in the system, with a diffuse basis of interest, so that the meaning in question cannot be treated as contingent on the fluctuating relations between the orienting actor and the environment.

There are noticeable differences between the pattern variables and the functional problems in this formulation. In conjunction with the four system problems, the pattern variables specify the particular modes of meaning and orientation necessary for the internal ordering of the system. However, the modes of meaning and orientation must shift if the system is to adapt to the environment.

The pattern variables have the further capacity of laying out the different orientations that must take place if the system is to maintain its "boundary" or "integrity" and thereby remain discriminated from the environment.

And now the pattern variables are indeed held to be exhaustive of all the possible combinations of general meanings and orientations that can occur.[20] However, Parsons' revision of the scheme he had worked out with Bales makes the scheme considerably more complicated. Where does "control" enter into any of the preceding? Perhaps Parsons' reformulation of his previously heralded "law of inertia" will give us one clue to this question:[21]

Change in the rate or direction of process is a consequence of disturbance in the relations between an actor or acting system and its situation, or the meaning of objects.

Another clue is to be found in Parsons' assertion that "the nature of the hierarchy of control . . . from the cultural . . . to the physical . . . (means) that the *structure* of systems of action is conceived as consisting of *patterns* of normative culture."[22] This is a critical part of Parsons' conception, but is not the only 'critical' part. Nevertheless, he underscores this idea several times by saying, for example, that "action theory is fundamentally oriented to the problem of *meaning* in the symbolic-cultural sense."[23] Does it follow from these clues that, should there be a change in the pattern of normative culture (that is, a change of meanings), there will be corresponding alterations throughout the entire action system? Will a cultural change 'produce' some sort of change in the social system it controls? Will a change in the social system have repercussions upon the personalities of its participating members? Will, finally, personality changes affect the behavioral organism? To think of the 'hierarchy of control' as a shock wave, so to speak, emanating from a cultural explosion is perhaps tempting but utterly inaccurate and misleading. Tempting, for this metaphor may induce a sense

[20] *Cf.* Parsons' claim in his answer to objections raised by Max Black, in "The Point of View of The Author," *op. cit.*, p. 330.

[21] "Pattern Variables Revisited," *op. cit.*, p. 481.

[22] *Ibid.*, p. 481.

[23] "The Point of View of the Author," *op. cit.*, p. 340.

that the relations between all the systems are really quite simple and may even be expressed in the form of causal statements. Misleading, however, because this metaphor entails a simple-minded reductionism which would abridge the integrity, the autonomy, of the social, personality and organismic systems. Parsons recognizes this very clearly. Consider his further comments:[24]

Social systems are dependent on the cultural systems which in part are institutionalized in them; but influence in the reverse direction is also crucially important . . . In a sense, a social system can be considered as suspended in a web of cultural definitions, whose pressures are by no means uniform or mutually coordinated in different directions. There may be an inherent direction of change in the meaning premises of the central value-system. The cognitive definitions of the system as object may be subject to many types of change or distortion. Commitments in different classes of personalities are not static. The relations of the society to the skills of the organism and the understanding of the environment are culturally patterned. In each of these contexts there is interaction and not merely a one-way process; and all the relevant factors have complex feedback effects on each other.

Our understanding of "control" is thus indeed most imprecise and remains to be amplified, perhaps, in the future. Except for the most rudimentary sorts of propositions that may be advanced, the relations between all the elements of any action system are yet unfathomed. If all human organisms perish, there will be no personalities, no social systems, and no cultures. If there is a culture there will be all the rest. If there is a social system the energies of the human organisms will have been directed towards solving the 'system problems' and adapting to an environment. The elements thus stand in a (necessary) 'conditional relationship' to one another. Parsons assumes as a matter of course that all these 'elements' are independent in some sense, that there is a lack of uniformity in cultural definition throughout a social system, and that between all the elements there will be 'complex feedback effects.' This is a more magnanimous conception than many other philosophies which, though narrower in purview, have been unable to render more precisely any of the relations envisioned between "infra" and "supra" structures without recourse to mere dogma. The manifold 'controls' that Parsons envisions, however, are hardly struck into instant transparency by a cybernetic metaphor. Promising though this metaphor may seem, it is no more at present than a metaphor whose promise has yet to be fulfilled.

To throw some light on these puzzlements, Parsons turns to another question: Are there identifiable prerequisites of certain major differentiations that have occurred in the structure of societies throughout history? Parsons has been interested in this question since his early work in the 1930's, as was suggested previously in chapter V. If I may refresh the reader's hopefully not overburdened memory, in *The Structure of Social Action* Parsons had declared that "action systems have properties that are emergent only on a certain level of complexity in the relations of (parts) to each other."[25] Now Parsons wishes to inquire more fully into a related question, to see whether certain "features of human societies at the level of culture and social organization (have) universal and major significance as prerequisites for socio-cultural development."[26] Perhaps we shall discern at least a few of the conditions for the emergence of certain levels of societal complexity.

Societal Evolution.—Parsons attacks the question with shades of his customary boldness, but the conceptual outcome is provisional and indecisive. I will review the materials and then conclude the chapter. The issues Parsons confronts are several. First, however simple or complex a society may be, it must be a recognizable society. That is, if Parsons is not to lapse into any version of historicism, relativism, or mere empiricism, his general definition of the 'social object' must be retained constantly throughout every variation of society he seeks to portray. By this 'theoretical device,' to borrow another of Althusser's figures of pertinence here, Parsons will ensure "that it really is a pudding we are eating and not a poached baby elephant, though we *think* we are eating our daily pudding."[27] But second, Parsons must also take precautions against lapsing into a 'mosaic theory of history' or a 'rigid evolutionary

[25] *Op. cit.*, p. 739.
[26] I, p. 356.
[27] *Op. cit.*, p. 57.

scheme.' If the variations of society he brings forth are cast as ideal-types, none of the societies will be 'comparable.' The only avenues then open to him are the 'mosaic' or rigid evolutionary routes by which he can attempt to order the ideal-types of societies—as he had pointed out thirty-years earlier (cited in chapter III). But what is wrong with these options?

A mosaic 'theory' of history allows us to wander in every direction and to see much, but our comprehension of what we have seen will then be composed of such a riot of tongues and an abundance of concepts, that our remembrance, and what we can say, will be choked into incoherence. A rigid evolutionary scheme carries us to the heights in an unswerving line from a single, lowly source, and thus beguiles us into the belief that we can survey everything and know the next step to be taken; but then, unexpectedly, the line veers to continue, perhaps, elsewhere; we take a mis-step, and dis-cover (sometimes bitterly) that our confidence has been riding upon an illusion. Parsons comes very close but wishes to avoid either of these alternatives. The difficulties which entrap him are of a different order. He wishes to see and to say everything, as it were, from a central source, neither high nor low but radiating in all directions at once. I do not think he has yet found a concept of sufficient centrality and potency to provide us with an unswerving sight of the many variations of society he seeks. But the interesting prospect implied is whether, even in the best of circumstances, he will have to broach some theory of history. For as variations of society occur in time and place, and as chronology and position are two of the fundaments of any historical conception, will there not be historical 'coördinates' involved whenever one thinks of societal variations? And if societal variations are somehow related to one another, will not the historical coördinates be related as well? So far as I know, neither Parsons nor anyone has as yet anything *new* to say on this matter that provides the slightest illumination, although formulae of 'synchrony' and 'diachrony' abound. Althusser, in the work cited, intimates that there is indeed a question here.

Because Parsons does not directly face the possible theory of history involved in his endeavor, his evolutionary notions are left exposed to severe, damaging criticism. Professor Nisbet, for example, has argued forcefully that Parsons' evolutionary idea, his 'metaphor' of growth and development, results in a linear classification of societal "stages" that is not applicable to any one society over any succeeding time intervals. This conception of sequence is therefore no more than a classification, and as an *evolutionary* idea is as deficient as the earlier notions of Comte, Morgan, Marx, Tylor, Spencer, et alia.[28] I agree there are parallels. Yet, given Parsons' epistemological premises, his endeavor is not devoid of interest. To put it in the simplest and most direct way I can, if we wish to study human beings in any way we of course must *know* we are studying human beings and not panda bears (or poached baby elephants). But if in our study we cannot tell the differences between human beings, our study will have amounted to very little. Are the differences between human beings merely differences *external* to them—differences in trees, huts, houses or skyscrapers? But human beings are not trees, huts and so on. Vary these externalia as much as we will, the external differences *alone* cannot make for the human differences. But then, what does? Our understanding of this question for human beings is minimal, and for societies perhaps less.

Parsons begins to suggest a few of the variations of society, although he has no clear idea of how they occur, or of the exact historical 'coördinates' applicable to any particular variation or sequence of variations. He offers us, tentatively, a few gross classificatory forms such as "primitive," "intermediate," and "modern." However, he also proposes "conditions" pertaining to these forms. Perhaps one day the propositions will lend themselves to a more precise backward glance. As I have already referred to the dilemmas of his 'stages' conception, I will confine my observations to the propositions that he gives us.

A prerequisite of major significance for socio-cultural development is called an "evolutionary universal." Parsons defines an evolutionary universal as "a complex of structures and associated processes the development of which so increases the long-run adaptive capacity of living organisms in a given class that only systems that develop the complex can attain certain higher levels of general adaptive

<hr>

[28] Nisbet, *Social Change and History*, *op. cit.*, ch. 8.

capacity.'[29] This does not mean that living systems without the 'complex' will necessarily be doomed to extinction; they may find an 'environmental niche' to accommodate them. For human life, the organic or physical prerequisites of adaptive evolution include such features as vision, an opposable thumb, and the human brain. Taken together, these physical features are necessary for the development of a recognizably human society even in the most primitive state. (The brain, for example, "is the organic basis of the capacity to learn and manipulate symbols."[30]) Nothing new here so far; these ideas have been expounded often in the work of many of the evolutionary biologists.[31] But Parsons' concern is no longer with the prerequisites of human society. He wishes to find the prerequisites of the development of human society once human society is an established fact.

For the simplest, most primitive action system, "religion (taken as the orientational aspect of culture), communication with language, social organization through kinship, and technology—may be regarded as an integrated set of evolutionary universals . . .'[32] Why so? Because "no human society has existed without *all* four in relatively definite relations to each other."[33] Social organization through kinship, for example, is made possible through the incest taboo which is universal to the nuclear family. Should the child not overcome his "infantile erotic attachments," he will not be motivated "to the higher order role-performance of the adult. In this connection, the incest taboo within the nuclear family has become perceived—in spite of certain peripheral exceptions—as a principal universal of human social organization and as very deeply involved in the motivational processes by which social systems are maintained."[34]

The extent to which Parsons relies on 'necessary reason'

---

[29] I, pp. 340–341; J, pp. 21, 26.
[30] I, p. 340; J, p. 32.
[31] *Cf.* George Gaylord Simpson, *The Meaning of Evolution* (New Haven: Yale University Press, 1950). Parsons refers to this work in his essay and in his short monograph.
[32] I, p. 342.
[33] I, *ibid.*; J, p. 32ff.
[34] H, vol. 1, p. 240; J, pp. 35–38.

wherever he turns is most striking. This form of reasoning is the single, most pervasive feature of his work, and I must call attention to this feature once again, and of the deficiencies of his work that are thereby entailed. If, without the incest taboo the child will not be motivated to the higher role performance of the adult, then even with the incest taboo we do not know why the child is ever motivated to this performance. The gap here between child and adult remains unbridged in Parsons' conception—except that when we see an adult we can infer that he must have been a child. This inference may give us small comfort. But we will now see the large comforts Parsons seeks to gain by this conceptual strategy. Briefly, the evolutionary universals are:

(1) If a society is to grow in numbers, and if the division of labor among its members is to become more complex, then a stratificational system not based on kinship ascription alone is a prerequisite for such growth, and for the superior coördination of the greater diversity of labor.[35]

(2) If political leadership is to institute *large* 'implementations,' and if such implementations are to be accepted as legitimate by the members of a society, then "legitimation" itself "must become a relatively explicit and, in many cases, a socially differentiated function." This means that, in addition to the requirement that the cultural basis of legitimation be made explicit, agencies independent of a diffuse religious tradition must be institutionalized to effect the "legitimation function."[36] This developmental prerequisite is referred to by Parsons simply as "cultural legitimation."

(3) If a society is to move considerably beyond a so-called "primitive" state, an additional evolutionary prerequisite is an administrative bureaucracy, particularly in government. For even a 'simple' bureaucracy with the accompanying trappings of literacy, a formal legal code, etc., "is the most effective large-scale administrative organization that man has invented, and there is no direct substitute for it. Where capacity to carry out large-scale organized operations is important, e.g., military operations with mass forces,

[35] I, pp. 342–345; J, p. 42ff.
[36] I, pp. 345–346; J, p. 47ff and ch. 5.

water control, tax administration, policing of large and heterogeneous populations, and productive enterprise requiring large
capital investment and much manpower, the unit that commands
effective bureaucratic organization is inherently superior to the one
that does not."[37]

(4) If the effective functioning of a collectivity is to be rapid, then
money and the market complex are two further evolutionary prerequisites. For, if power is not concentrated, say, in a bureaucracy,
that bureaucracy cannot operate swiftly. "Power is in part a function
of the mobility of the resources available for use in the interests of
the collective goals in question." Money is the most mobile of such
resources. But "mobility of resources . . . is a direct function of access
to them through the market." Money and markets are placed above
bureaucracies in the hierarchical series of developmental requisites,
for "the conditions of their large scale development are more pre-
carious." However, generally "money (and markets have) undoubtedly made a fundamental contribution to the adaptive capacity
of the societies in which (they) have developed . . .". Societies that
restrict these requisites too "drastically are likely to suffer severe
disadvantages in the long run."[38]

(5) If vast areas of social life are to become involved in bureaucracies and markets, then bureaucratic and market systems must be
guided by universalistic norms. "For bureaucracy, these (norms)
involve definitions of the powers of office, the terms of access (to
office), and the line dividing proper from improper pressure or
influence. For money and markets, the relevant norms include the
whole complex of property rights, first in commodities, later in land
and in monetary assets . . . Although it is difficult to pin down just
what the crucial components are, how they are interrelated, and
how they develop, one can identify the development of a general
legal system as a crucial aspect of societal evolution. A general legal
system is an integrated system of universalistic norms, applicable to
the society as a whole . . ." Bureaucracies may develop without a
highly generalized, universalistic, normative order, but development will then be limited. Parsons suggests that the "English type

[37] I, pp. 347–348; J, pp. 45, 51, 52ff.
[38] I, pp. 349–350.

of legal system (was) a fundamental prerequisite of the first occurrence of the Industrial Revolution."[39]

(6) If the polity is to be effective in a large scale society, then the development of a democratic association is a prerequisite. For "political effectiveness," says Parsons, "includes both the scale and operative flexibility of the organization of power. Power, however, as a generalized societal medium, depends overwhelmingly on a consensual element, i.e., the ordered institutionalization and exercise of influence, linking the power system to the high-order societal consensus at the value-level."[40]

Parsons' depiction of this series of evolutionary universals is admittedly sketchy and programmatic. Except for the obvious fact that we have no knowledge of how these various societal forms come into being, we can see the basis of their formulation. First, each of the evolutionary necessities is a modality of one or another functional sub-system. Second, we gain a slightly clearer sense—if only in the examples—of what Parsons is after when he refers to the hierarchy of control. Parsons believes that however socio-cultural innovations may occur, they will not occur "automatically with increases of factors or resources at the lower (conditional) levels of the cybernetic hierarchies...(For) essential as a large population may be for advanced social organization, the pressure of increasing numbers alone cannot create such an organization—rather, it will release Malthusian checks. Properly developed, this argument also applies to economic productivity and political power."[41]

Notice, therefore, that the list of general necessities has increased once again. I should like now to note them quickly to mark the turning points in Parsons' thought and to summarize my argument. First, the categories of the means-end framework were proposed as logically necessary for all social thought. Then, each of the functional sub-systems was conceived to be necessary to any social system. To all of this was added the conditions of structural and temporal differentiation of the units of any social system held to be necessary for the existence of the system. Following, there was proposed the

[39] I, pp. 350–353.
[40] I, pp. 353–356.
[41] J, p. 113.

'hierarchy of cybernetic control' as an ingredient apparently necessary (though vaguely stated) to organize the sub-systems of any societal system. And presently—although we have no idea whether this will be the end of it all—the modalities of society are not merely logically construed combinations of the elements, but are conceived to occur in a necessary temporal sequence: certain variations of society cannot occur before the others. Almost every one of the conditional necessities Parsons has brought forth has led him to revise his logical framework of action—to add to or emend the categories of that framework in some way. But if Parsons is to combat relativism by his own standards, must he not show that he can ground his framework of action without further alteration, and that once grounded it will be commodious enough to accommodate any further possible general necessities that may be found or conceived? If he cannot do this, his framework will not be a perfectly stationary "non-relative" point into which *all* other social theories may be translated.

Is it possible that Parsons has quietly abandoned the fight against relativism, and is no longer concerned with unifying social knowledge? in 1961 Parsons had noted that the concept of social evolution was antithetical to the "anti-evolutionist trend and the methodological positions deriving from German Idealist 'historicism,'" for such methodological positions emphasized the relativity and incomparability of cultures.[42] Now, at the close of his short monograph on evolution, published in 1966, Parsons again states that "great confusion . . . has arisen from the dogma, often left implicit, that evolutionary theory must be 'historical' in the sense of historic*ism*. Whether following Hegel, Marx, or later Germans such as Dilthey, historicism has characteristically denied the possibility or relevance of generalized *analytical* theory (which systematically treats the interdependence of independently variable factors) in explaining temporally sequential socio-cultural phenomena."[43]

If Parsons is opposed—epistemologically—to a narrowly conceived Marxism, he is equally opposed to any narrow view of society including those views launched under "conservative" auspices. Notice what he says of Dilthey. The ideological critiques miss this

[42] H, vol. 1, p. 240; J, pp. 114–115.
[43] J, p. 115.

aspect of his work entirely. For Parsons wishes to incorporate and transform every narrow view into a single overarching conception which will allow us to behold, eventually, every variation of society that can exist. There remains a huge gap between his intention and his achievement. And whether his intention can ever be fulfilled is a subject best left to soothsayers. But there is no doubt that there is a constancy in his work that does not come solely from his interests in the 'problem of social order,' or the conditions of societal equilibrium. Parsons has remained true to the epistemological vision expressed in his first major work. I shall conclude this study with a few comments on that vision.

CHAPTER EIGHT

Conclusion:
On Unification of Social Knowledge

Parsons has labored mightily to conceive a concept of the social that will be at once supremely general and also discriminating of the many varieties of society that have existed. His labors have been far from fruitless, but they have not yet issued, as we have seen, in the concept he wants. Whether a single, social concept can ever be conceived that will possess all the characteristics Parsons deems desirable —inclusiveness, universality, irreducibility necessity, stability, logical rigor, and causal explanatory power of the covering law type—is, I think, doubtful. I will not argue the point. But let me ask: does a single concept presently reign in any domain of scientific knowledge? We know that Kant's own far more complex and rigorous scheme of the a priori categories, great an achievement though it was, has been found limited. Kant meant his categories to apply to the Newtonian physics which he believed to be the sole, unshakable science of the physical world. He thus believed his categories to be equally unshakable and inclusive. But the Kantian categories do not include, for example, the a priori concept of four-dimensional space, as Whitehead dubbed it, applicable to relativity physics.[1] I do not mean to hold up the fact that Kant's scheme is not all-inclusive in order to fault Parsons' endeavors! The analogy is indeed too far afield. Physics is not sociology. But as Kant's a priori scheme does provide Parsons with an analogy of sorts, this very analogy may serve to make an important distinction.

A large part of the value and point of an epistemological analysis, for those who seek knowledge, is to bring us to a closer recognition of "the field," to the kinds of concepts and principles available to our understanding at a given moment by which we distinguish and

---

[1] *The Concept of Nature, op. cit.*

L

pursue our rational objectives. Philosophy of science, as commonly understood, does not exhaust epistemology. For epistemological analysis attempts to clarify the various meanings of knowledge, and to arrive ultimately at a concept of all the meanings of knowledge. And surely there are *various* meanings of knowledge: physics is not sociology, logic is not physics, and so on. How may we understand the differences? There are of course many principles applicable to all 'fields'; our understanding is not segregated, as it were, into so many air-tight compartments. Very few, I should think, willingly court contradiction—to mention one obvious logical restriction held, with few exceptions, to pertain to all domains of knowledge. 'Concepts without percepts are empty' is another famous theorem of a different order, argued by Kant to apply to every sphere of knowledge. And there are many more. Let us agree with Levi-Strauss, whose dictum was cited near the beginning of this study, that 'object' and 'method' are not the same things. Does it follow that there is a perfect unity of methods and principles equally applicable to the most heterogeneous of 'objects'?

Parsons has never once flagged in distinguishing the physical from the cultural, personality systems from organismic systems, etc. Each term is meant to designate a distinct class of objects. And to each class, in turn, there is a distinctive principle by which the objects of that class are interrelated. Consistency, Parsons says, is the principle appropriate to cultural objects, or to meanings. Causality is the principle appropriate to physical objects, or 'things.' But there are yet further principles by which classes of objects may themselves be interrelated. Teleology—or 'purpose'—and this term need not be construed in a metaphysical or religious light—is the principle that applies at least to the human organism. For the human organism, as an 'object,' is not exclusively a 'thing.' Every human organism has cultural and also physical attributes. Stones do not speak or strive. 'Action is...the process of alteration of the conditional elements in the direction of conformity with norms," we will recall Parsons having said.[2] Can the same general principles required to comprehend the nature and relations of physical objects allow us fully to comprehend the nature and relations of speaking and

[2] *The Structure of Social Action, op. cit.*, p. 733.

striving 'objects'? This question, simply and rather bluntly put, is at the center of much of the epistemological storm that has raged in modern social thought, the positive and the negative answers signifying the several 'metaphysical' standpoints. Perhaps Chomsky is right in saying that if any of the negative answers to this question also succeeds in providing us with clear and firm 'non-physical' principles or laws for the comprehension of speaking and striving 'objects,' there may well be an extension of our concept of 'physical explanation' to accommodate and incorporate such new principles.[3] Epistemological analysis never ends. The epistemological controversies of the nineteenth and early twentieth centuries have been well documented, especially in the works of Ernst Cassirer that have been cited, and will not be pursued here. Parsons' response to this question, as we have seen, is that no one class of objects may be absorbed by another. Each class of objects is irreducible. But this is not indeed his entire response, and if we examine his response with care we shall find, I think, that it is vacillating and ambiguous.

The locus of Parsons' equivocation is to be found in his discussions of the determinants or principles that relate all the classes of objects which make up society. In his first major work Parsons says he aims to reach a 'science' of social action. But he does not use the term 'science' in the generic sense of knowledge. He wishes to find *causal laws* to relate all concrete social facts. Neither positivist nor historicist standpoints are adequate, Parsons believes, to the task he has set. Let us look quickly at his reasons once again. Positivist explanations, as they are causal, embody the 'correct logical form,' Parsons seems to think, but stem from a concept too meager to enfold all the objects pertinent to social action. We know the positivist concept is too meager, Parsons argues, for every effort to 'derive' a causal explanation of the facts of social action from positivist premises has so far failed. Historicist assertions are, by virtue of their extreme idiography of statement and the peculiarity of their 'Verstehen' methods, doomed to be forever faulty for the purposes of causal explanation. But the historicists also refer to a necessary part of social action.

There are two assumptions here which bear repeating. The first is

[3] *Language and Mind, op. cit.*, pp. 83–84.

that universal laws are required for a causal explanation. As mentioned at several previous points, this assumption seems to endorse the well known, acclaimed, and often discussed covering-law or subsumption model of explanation. The covering-law model involves a distinctive logical pattern corresponding to the enthymeme whose upshot in empirical cognitions has been likened to a 'prediction.' The second assumption seems to be, then, that the covering law model is itself a requirement of empirical knowledge which the historicists fail to meet, for the *determination* of empirical knowledge is based on a causal principle expressed exclusively through causal laws. It is widely held that some causal principle, whose laws are not necessarily reductionist in content, is involved in the determination of empirical facts. Under these assumptions, for example, Hempel has argued that historical studies are at best striking "explanation sketches." The causal laws involved in historical studies, suggests Hempel, are of such inordinate complexity that they have not yet been formulated with sufficient clarity to fulfill the tenets of the covering-law model of explanation.[4] Parsons made a similar point rather earlier than Hempel, if we will remember, in his discussion of Ranke. How then, if causal laws are an explicit requirement of the ordering of empirical facts, even an 'explanation sketch' without the clear use of causal laws is possible, remains something of a mystery. For can we find covering-laws of any kind —reduced or unreduced, vague or opaque—in the historical studies to which Hempel and Parsons refer? We may even begin to suspect that historical studies are an assortment of materials without rhyme or reason—a collection, as it were, of so much debris. Neither Hempel nor Parsons has ever suggested this, for they seek to formulate a dilemma rather than dismiss a discipline.

The ambiguities and indeed uncertainties in all of this, as has been argued in many recent discussions, are whether universal laws are in fact required for a causal explanation, and whether every determination of empirical matters must in fact be a 'causal' determination. The ambiguities do not hinge merely on a definition of

[4] "The Function of General Laws in History," in Herbert Feigl and Wilfrid Sellars (ed.), *Readings in Philosophical Analysis* (New York: Appelton-Century-Crofts, inc., 1949), pp. 459–471.

cause but on the question of the differences in logical patterns of explanation when there is an interest in seeking other than causal
determinations of empirical facts. Are other 'non-lawful' determinations possible, and what would they be? We know that in ancient
times Aristotle raised a form of this question in his conception of
teleology. Recently, however, philosophers have again posed the
question, without metaphysical intent but with perhaps greater
logical precision.[5] I shall soon glance at a few of the more recent
views, for I believe they are of considerable importance to the
methodology of the social sciences. In any case, I have attempted to
show that as Parsons' work does not succeed in providing us with
the 'causal knowledge' he apparently seeks, the work is 'inadequate'
on 'internal' grounds. But I believe the assumptions are too
restrictive. And I believe also that despite all of Parsons' statements
that may be taken to show he endorses these assumptions, his work
reveals that he conceives other than causal determinations of the
concrete facts of social action. If the assumptions can be challenged,
or placed into doubt, the binding claims Parsons means to establish
by these assumptions may be broken—or at least loosened. To loosen
the assumptions will mean they may have a qualified or limited
applicability.

As evidence that Parsons' attitude towards these assumptions is
at least unclear, notice that his early work terminates in a voluntaristic view of man. In his early work Parsons conceives a philosophy
of man as a creative being constituting himself and his society over
and again with every one of his morally creative actions, and yet
never once departing from the natural world. The notion of the
creativity of man defies causal explanation as conventionally understood, but is not antithetical to some kind of determination. The
determination Parsons attempts to establish in his early work
is not merely a causal but a 'rationalist' determination. The
logical categories of his means-end framework underlie our comprehension of man's actions and purposes, however free or creative

---

[5] *Cf.* Charles Taylor, *The Explanation of Behaviour* (London: Routledge &
Kegan Paul, 1964); G. E. M. Anscombe, *Intention* (Oxford: Basil Blackwell,
1957); and Georg Henrik von Wright, *Explanation and Understanding*
(London: Routledge & Kegan Paul, 1971).

they may be. We can therefore begin to understand our own actions and purposes, not psychologically—through sympathetic intuition (or 'Verstehen')—but semantically through the concepts of their meaning and intention. Our own actions may thus become intelligible, or conceptually determinate, to us. Here Parsons approaches an epistemology of intention and interpretation rather than an epistemology geared exclusively to social causation. He believes, however, that any determination—causal, interpretive, intentional—will require universal categories and laws of some kind. In this light, he considers his later functional scheme to be only 'second best.'

If one assumes the various classes of 'objects' to which Parsons refers are present in any human society—which I should think is beyond question—there is truly a great puzzle as to how they are related. There is equally as great a puzzle as to how our conceptions of these objects are to be related. But that the puzzle may not be unlocked by one conceptual key is exactly the argument Parsons advances against the reductionisms of the philosophical schools. Why then should we think a single methodological key will do the job? Whether the job can be done is most uncertain, painful as this prospect may seem, for the numerous keys available to us may be grounded in ways too irreconcilable for any formula to breach. Perhaps a solution of sorts will be found not in a master key, and not in a simple opposition of one key to another, but in making all the keys equally accessible to us. And this may result in a 'dialectical' poise in its own right whose tensions, however, are not held in synthesis by anything remotely resembling a Hegelian dialectic. I shall take up this theme later.

For the moment, let me note that Parsons appears to use the term 'causal explanation' in a broad way to refer to any kind of lawful or analytical determination of an empirical fact. In his interesting but brief essay of 1965 on "Unity and Diversity in the Modern Intellectual Disciplines,"[6] he draws the distinction between the disciplines of natural and social science with respect to the 'objects' of their interests. But he believes these disciplines nevertheless achieve a kind of methodological unity, for they resort equally to analytical and generalized theory and rely upon a 'causal category' as well.

[6] *Daedalus*, Winter 1965, vol. 94, #1, pp. 39–65.

If the differences in meaning of 'causal category' are more than merely terminological, however, it would be important to bring these differences out. For we must consider whether a methodological issue has been obscured by the ready equation: cause = law. This issue pertains to the logic of the relations between 'subject' and 'object.' And the question is whether there are significant differences, not merely in the 'objects' of the several intellectual disciplines, but in the distinctive methods by which these disciplines appropriate their objects and thus attempt to bridge the gulf almost every scholar since Descartes has assumed to exist between "subject" and "object." I shall take up these questions very briefly but with the aim of pointing to genuine possibilities which have been overlooked by the general sweep of many of the claims that have been made.

Rational Determinations of Empirical Facts.—My discussion will be untechnical but will draw from sources where a much richer and far more rigorous treatment of the issues may be found. The belief that 'being caused' is an instance of a universal law is, as Professor Anscombe has recently observed, more of a *Weltanschauung* rather than a conviction exclusive to one philosophical school.[7] Hempel's presentation of the covering-law model is an elegant expression of this belief, although his analysis is couched primarily to the natural sciences and he has undoubtedly been inspired by the philosophy of positivism. The question is not whether 'being caused' is utterly unrelated to a universal law—which would be, at the least, difficult to maintain. The question is, rather, whether being caused *must* be related to a universal law. To this question Anscombe has replied with a number of interesting observations on human interference and prevention. Some of her points are that we can know causes without knowing what is involved in causation, and that by the 'interferences' of an experiment we may discover scientific laws. However, Parsons and apparently Hempel, among many others, answer the question at issue unblinkingly in the affirmative. Accordingly, it has seemed to follow that the logical proof of something being caused, and thus the determination of that thing, must

---

[7] "Causality and Determination," *An Inaugural Lecture* (Cambridge: The University Press, 1971).

conform to a syllogism of which the enthymeme is *the* exemplar. As Hempel's version of this form of proof has been cited and reprinted many times in the social science literature, I will assume the reader's familiarity and so will not reproduce it.

Another implication follows which is obvious and bedevilling: apparently, there are no possible 'explanation models' other than the subsumption model that would be available to the empirical sciences. Given this implication, the bedevilment consists in the fact that the social sciences and historical studies (and many of the natural sciences?) must be seen to explain nothing. For these disciplines do not have the resources, the constant 'laws,' to employ the model. The conclusion is inescapable, although one may doubt whether it is widely believed.

The recent studies by Anscombe and von Wright suggest that there is an 'explanation model' available to the social sciences of a different character from the enthymeme. They call this model the 'practical syllogism.' This syllogism would appear to be simplicity itself, although there are logical problems. As Professor von Wright has discussed these matters with great care, it will be sufficient for my purposes merely to cite the 'model' and point to a few of the implications which may help to give us some perspective on supremely generalized conceptions. *A highly simplified* example of a practical argument would be:

(1) Mr X, who has just entered the railway station, intends to board a train which is due to leave in four minutes.

(2) He considers that the distance between himself and the train is such that he must run if he is to catch the train on time.

(3) Mr X thus sets himself to running.

The 'explanation' of Mr X's running appears patent. However, the very first thing to observe in the argument is that the "conclusion" (3) does not follow from the premises. The premises "do not entail the 'existence' of a conclusion to match them. The syllogism when leading up to action is 'practical' and not a piece of logical demonstration. It is only when action is already there and a practical argument is constructed to explain or justify it that we have a logically conclusive argument. The necessity of the practical inference schema is, one could say, a necessity conceived *ex post actu*."[8] Observe, then, that the practical syllogism predicts nothing, for whatever is determined by this form of reasoning is not 'predetermined' but is, so to speak, 'postdetermined.'

Perhaps the very ubiquity of our thinking in a way similar to the practical syllogism has blinded us to the fact that the logical pattern of this kind of reasoning is distinctive. Although the form of this reasoning may appear obvious, the question of the entailment of the inference of a practical argument is complex and may yet be open to further analysis. But if, as Professor von Wright believes he has shown, the practical argument is a valid logical form, it follows that the validity of this form of reasoning does not necessarily require general premises. And if this is the case, *one* of the arguments Parsons has advanced against the explanatory shortcomings of the 'historical school' may be challenged. For not only is it possible to employ *concepts* of very narrow scope but, most importantly, it is also possible to make logically valid *relational* statements when using such concepts. The reader will recall the discussion of the second chapter: Parsons believes that without general categories and rules the alleged 'facts' of empirical studies cannot be related and will thus remain an unordered aggregate. I think the arguments of Anscombe and von Wright place this belief into doubt. On the other hand, there is no license now granted for an unbridled empiricism. The reasons for doubting Parsons' belief and for opposing a simple empiricism may be made clearer by exploring a few characteristics of the practical argument.

Let us assume the form of the argument is valid. This assumption of course does not bring us to conclude the substance of the argument is empirically (or materially) correct. Evidence must be marshalled and tested to decide the latter question. Moreover, alternative interpretations of the activity may be expected. An activity that is of broad interest may elicit a great many possible alternative explanations some of which will perhaps adduce evidence more clearly and amply than others. All of this is important and incontestable. What may be brought to the reader's attention, however, is that in the example of the practical argument the explanation is not causal but teleological. For the behavior in question—running to catch the train

[8] von Wright, *ibid.*, p. 117

—is *described* as intentional, and can thus be understood by referring to a future state of affairs Mr. X is desirous of obtaining. That future is not 'in' the running. And the desired future may never come to pass whatever Mr. X does. But whether or not Mr X reaches his goal, the *conceptual* relations between his activity and his intentions allow us to explain his running 'teleologically.'

A teleological explanation of human activity thus depends first and foremost upon an explication of meaning. In the example given, the significance Mr. X attaches to his running must be brought out. His activity may be open to several interpretations. Perhaps he is one of that breed of enthusiasts who seek exercise upon the slightest opportunity and would run for his train in almost any event. On this occasion he may run with confidence but he runs to 'catch' the train on time. Intentions and activities may be distinguished, classified and opposed. But as there is no reason to assume intentions and activities will be all of a kind, so there is no reason to assume that each may not be the only one of its kind. (I think Parsons is brought to the latter assumption by his argument). To explicate the meaning of a *complex* human activity will thus require the most searching examination and cross-examination. There is nothing mysterious in this for any human activity, although I do not mean to minimize the difficulties involved. There is a condition, as it were, which makes this kind of knowledge possible: "we cannot understand or teleologically explain behavior which is completely alien to us."[9] And if we could not decipher any aspect of the thought and language of a group of human beings—say, in the distant past—the significance *they* may have placed upon their activities would then be otiose to us. If we know something of their activities, however, we could venture an interpretation. Once expressed conceptually, an interpretation of the meanings and purposes of a human activity may be arranged into an explanatory 'network,' so to say, of practical arguments. This is one way human activity may be rationally determined without employing general concepts. Often, but not always, these sorts of determinations are found in historical studies.

None of the preceding is meant to deny the obvious fact that human beings have some purposes in common, or that groups of

[9] von Wright, *ibid.*, p. 114.

human beings—not merely individuals—may be distinguished from one another. The activities of a particular collectivity of human beings have a meaning which is not easily identified with the meaning of the activities of the discrete individuals who compose the group. Perhaps by 'extracting' the intentions of the individual members we may come to understand the significance of the group. Nevertheless, it is in the meaning and significance of the group's activities, as a group, that the sociologist and historian has a primary interest, and for which he seeks an explanation. These elementary considerations point up the fact that the example given of the practical argument is no more than an example. It is the form of the argument that is important.

Parsons would be the first to agree that teleology is fundamental to the 'objects' of the social sciences. But he would wish to ground all singular teleological statements. For in addition to his concern with establishing the possibility of social knowledge (general categories, universal laws), he is also concerned with overcoming relativism. I shall examine this question very soon. The kinds of constructions Parsons wants to give to human intentions are, in von Wright's terminology, 'quasi-teleological.' They are teleological as they take due account of the intentional aspects of human life. But they would be quasi-teleological if they (succeed to) render these aspects with universal necessity (if never that, never this). The distinction is useful.

Very much the same principle of distinction may be applied usefully when speaking of causation. A 'quasi-causal' account would not involve universal laws; but a causal explanation would indeed involve universal laws. Why did the vase topple? The cat knocked it over. We place the vase back on the table and shush the cat. But now the cat hurls itself with demoniacal fury upon the vase. The vase remains stationary. We may be surprised by this fact, but it is not unthinkable and would not be indescribable if it were to occur. A Newtonian law may be broken, perhaps we suppose, but that would not prevent us from searching for the cause of the vases's fixity on this occasion. We could in fact speak of that cause and this effect without presupposing there is a universal and necessary connection between them, such that, whenever that cause, this effect.

However, were we to indulge ourselves in this presupposition without doing many other very complicated things, such as experimenting and trying to discover what the law may be, if there is any, there should be no good reason for anyone to humor our indulgence. Whether there is a law involved whenever a physical fact occurs, then, cannot be assumed in advance of our finding that law. Our own actions are of the first importance in this search. Not having the law at our disposal does not prevent us from making singular causal statements. (The reader may profitably consult the writings of Anscombe, Taylor, and von Wright, and of many others whom they cite, for a far more developed account of this bare argument).

If we assume that laws are not necessarily involved, how would we strike the distinction between a 'quasi-causal' and a 'teleological' relation? The relation between an act and an intention is conceptual and logical; between a singular cause and a singular effect, we usually say, is 'physical.' Why physical? The cause happens, the effect is achieved. Cause and effect are held to be extrinsic and logically unconnected, whereas action and intention are held to be intrinsic and logically involved with one another. An intention does not 'cause' the act, for the act in question is described as intentional. The intentions that we formulate as premises to a practical argument may be incorrect, but this matter could be clarified by an empirical investigation.

The distinctions help, I think, not only to demarcate the 'objects' that we study but also to differentiate the meaning of the 'causal category' upon which Parsons, in company with many others, believes the natural and social sciences rely. If the term 'causal category' is to be used, some recognition should be given to the differences in the 'determinations' of the 'objects' the several intellectual disciplines attempt to establish. This does not imply in the least that physical happenings are unimportant to the investigations of social scientists. As we have seen, Parsons has been emphatic that physical facts—such as technology, food supply, or the biological aspects of the organism—are important solely as conditions. Physical facts, he has asserted repeatedly, do not 'explain' or subsume human actions. There is implicit in Parsons' emphasis a recognition that 'teleology' itself cannot be caused. In fact, teleological and causal relations, as defined previously, would seem to be irreconcilable as they proceed from utterly dissimilar grounds. But an explanation of a series of human actions would not then be incoherent if in that explanation there is a mixture of quasi-causal statements and practical arguments. Human beings interpret events in the natural and social worlds.

Parsons' point is thus sometimes blurred when he speaks undiscriminatingly of a 'causal category.' There is, furthermore, a small strand of conceptual confusion that runs through much of the action schema. The confusion is made up in part of Parsons' amorphous conception of causality and also of his belief that the occurrence of a physical fact is an instance of a 'law' or a general principle of some kind. The pleasure principle, he has said, "is a feature of the organism which we know by experience we can count on to operate in certain ways, and which hence belongs analytically to the conditions of action."[10] Over and again, as was brought out in the second chapter, Parsons has said that a 'condition' is something we can *always* rely on (whereas man is a creative being), and that positivist thought gives us the important knowledge of such conditions. Now notice the 'hence' in the quoted statement. And consider that one may seriously entertain 'indeterministic' ideas, as intimated above. Then would it mean that if we could not 'count on' a feature of the organism to operate in certain ways we would be unsure where that feature belongs (categorically)? I doubt Parsons would want to say anything like this at all. But if the standard he seems to be using here when defining a 'condition' is compared to his ultimate conceptual goal—the lawful, causal determination of social action—all the elements of the action schema will fall into the conditions of action when they are explained 'causally.' For then we will be able to count on ends, means, norms and conditions alike to be operating in certain ways. This curious and unlikely outcome of his thought is rooted in his unstable amalgam of positivist and 'historical' premises. And it is precisely this instability that leads to the ambiguity, referred to earlier, in Parsons' conception of the determinants relating all the classes of elements pertaining to human, social life.

[10] *The Structure of Social Action, op. cit.*, p. 64.

When we look beyond his programmatic statements to his substantive work another picture emerges. He is concerned with determinations, but they are no longer 'causal.' He does not seek the 'predeterminations' of social life. He does not try to tell us what must be but what must have been. We have seen in his pervasive employment of necessary reasoning that Parsons seeks 'post-determinations' of social activity, and the quasi-teleological elements in his thinking are thus most prominent. Meanings, normative regulations, conceptions of the desirable are among the chief premises in his attempt to explain social action. *Only* in the sense of "emphasizing the importance of the cybernetically highest elements in patterning action systems," Parsons says in his monograph on social evolution, "I am a cultural determinist rather than a social determinist."[11] Whether fundamental principles of cultural diversity can be found, and universal laws discovered that will link the cultural to the conditional components of social life—is perhaps open. However, there is a related question for which a general answer may be supplied. The question is, how do we come to know we can rely on something to be 'operating' in certain ways? An answer consistent with Parsons' premises would be that we can know only by our own actions, our own interferences with nature, in which we strive to move the conditional elements in a direction of 'conformity with norms.' Does this mean we can know ourselves, and count on our norms and intentions to be operating in a certain way, only by our own actions, our 'interferences' with society? But then we must look to the past for some sort of answer to this question, for it is only in history that our own actions have occurred.

Relativism.—We now approach the dragon's lair. The difficulties are not to be taken lightly, but they have been made almost unbearable by a tacit merging of two, distinct questions. I shall attempt swiftly to separate them, but do not pretend to overcome the obstacles. When Parsons examines the many explanations of human activity for which there is some evidence he asks essentially one question: how much of human activity is explained by any single view? His concern is not to challenge the "truth" of any of the

[11] *Societies: Evolutionary and Comparative Perspectives, op. cit.,* p. 113.

explanatory schemes that are of interest to him, for he considers they have been verified to an extent or they would be lacking in scientific import. His concern, rather, is to challenge the over-riding claims often made by the proponents of these several explanatory views, and to develop standards to gauge the range of application of any one view. The question of validity, as discussed in the third chapter, becomes in Parsons' treatment not a question of "truth" but of the extent of truth—or of the comprehensiveness of any view. To put it very simply, he is of the conviction few are likely to oppose, that more truths are preferable to less. This conviction is congruent with his interest in 'cumulating empirical findings.' Parsons' endeavor to formulate a scheme into which all other social theories may be 'translated' is thus an attempt to provide the most extensive conception of social knowledge. Commendable as this may be, it has nothing to do with validity. More truths are being sought, but not truth. He would certainly not attempt to 'translate' social falsehoods into his scheme. What follows from this is that if some 'verified' explanation of social activity cannot be translated into Parsons' scheme, his scheme must be judged to be less than fully comprehensive. The scheme is not thereby 'invalidated,' but a limit to the purview of the scheme can be established.

There is some difficulty, however, in coming to a precise judgement of the limits of Parsons' theoretical work. If we look only at the several frameworks he has developed, we see immediately they are pitched to such an extremely general level as to accommodate very much that has been said ('truly' let us suppose) of social life. Consider the means-end scheme, for it is simpler than his later frameworks. Any social or historical study can be shown to presuppose some or all of the categories of that scheme. The means-end framework, he has said, has an 'epistemological' rather than an explanatory function. Are there perhaps certain categories to which Parsons' framework is insensitive?

Consider most briefly his later work. We have seen that it is of great importance to Parsons to be able to integrate his framework with any specialized study, say, of the functional sub-systems of groups and societies. The reason this is so important to him is that he must show his framework can indeed "translate" well and rigorously, and thus provide a genuine basis for the accretion of social knowledge. It is not enough to say the "same" categories are presupposed in all social inquiry. What does the 'same' mean? For if any version of his frameworks cannot detect nuances of the categories he believes are basic, the fertility and the epistemological precision of those frameworks will be placed into question. A gloss may be made of one or another mode of these categories that will then be difficult to assess—granting Parsons' assumptions. Indeed, we have yet to see, for example, whether there are any items of the action framework that will allow for the 'derivation' (or translation) of one of Parsons' own later findings, namely, the necessary sequence of societal modalities postulated in his evolutionary scheme.

The major difficulty, therefore, in arriving at an estimate of the possible limits of Parsons' scheme is that the scheme itself has not been sufficiently developed. It seems to have many possibilities. But will an alteration of his framework be required to encompass a a possible theory of the 'cybernetic hierarchy'? The question cannot be prejudged. But we cannot yet tell whether the latest version of the framework is richly enough conceived so that specialized studies of social activities now available can be brought into coherence with his framework. Everything awaits further developments. Does this mean, then, we are presently left to flounder in the warfare of many antagonistic explanations and interpretations of social life or are we forced to choose among them? How shall we choose?

There is and there has been a procedure available that will enable us to come to a *rational* judgement of any view. It is in fact very ancient. That procedure will even enable us to retrieve judgements we recognize have been faulty. Criticism is required, never-ending, intensive, searching criticism. It is not less talk that we want but more talk. It is not the posing of one view to the exclusion of all others—Marxism versus functionalism versus behavioralism, say— but the contesting and challenging of one viewpoint by another so that we may assess the strengths and weaknesses of every view. A higher viewpoint may never be attained. And every view cannot be assumed to be as 'good' as any other—a levelling relativism— but we can hope to find those views that are better than others for certain of our rational purposes. The result of criticism at any one time may then well be an apparent 'eclecticism' of views. This should not be very troubling to us, for at least the resources of the explanatory standpoints available may be better understood. And if better understood and in closer coördination to our rational pursuits, how 'eclectic' then will the possession of many viewpoints be? A certain degree of skepticism has always been beneficial for the raising of questions. And this too is involved in the pursuit of knowledge.

It is in the spirit of these comments that I have undertaken this study of a few aspects of perhaps the most important body of sociological thought to have emerged in the last four decades.

M

Index